Jesus Outside the Lines is a refreshing look at discipleship in our late modern times. While it's impossible to cover all the possible topics, Scott's book is still surprisingly comprehensive and readable at the same time. He seamlessly weaves together theology, cultural critique, Christian ethics, and character formation in each chapter. The result is a picture of Christian living that should be attractive to believers and to many skeptics as well.

TIMOTHY KELLER
Senior pastor of Redeemer Presbyterian Church, New York City, and author of *The Reason for God: Belief in an Age of Skepticism*

As people who have wrestled much with God's habit of redemptively "coloring outside the lines" in our own lives and experience, we are so grateful for the wisdom, care, and honesty with which our friend and pastor Scott Sauls has approached this subject in this book.

STEVEN CURTIS AND MARY BETH CHAPMAN
Five-time Grammy winners and orphan-care advocates

In an increasingly loud, polarizing world that finds itself in this confusing, prevailing "culture of outrage," of these us-against-them conversations about sexuality, politics, race, money, injustice, religion, Scott has written one of the most needed books of our times, one that I fervently believe should be in the hands of every single Christian without exception. Utterly weary of us-against-them and not sure of the way forward? This is an absolute must-read that I cannot recommend highly enough. One of the best, needed, reads of the year.

ANN VOSKAMP
Author of *One Thousand Gifts: A Dare to Live Fully Right Where You Are*

Scott Sauls has given me fresh hope in this thoughtful and lively book, *Jesus Outside the Lines*. He describes hope as imagining God's future into the present and does just that. He gives us a new way of relating to each other inside the church—especially on divisive topics related to our politics and commitments—in hopes of sweeter aroma to those who don't know Jesus. And he prods us to engage the issues of the world we live in—poverty, abortion, sexual "freedom," and selfish ambition, to name a few—with humility and love. It's so easy to be discouraged by the broken state of the church and the world, but Scott reminds us that God's once-and-for-all restoration project has already begun. We only need to believe that gospel!

KATHERINE LEARY ALSDORF
Founder and director emeritus, Redeemer Center for Faith & Work, and co-author of *Every Good Endeavor*

As a public official, I am often painfully aware of the church's tendency to want to paint lines that divide rather than drawing pictures of a life-giving Savior. As an exemplary model of speaking truth in love, Scott is a refreshing alternative to this. I am among many who have the privilege of trying to figure out how to do this alongside him.

BILL HASLAM
Governor of Tennessee

My pastor and friend, Scott Sauls, thoughtfully challenges the instinct to retreat or compromise when perspectives collide. With grace and humility, he calls us to press in and engage those whose perspectives are different than our own. If you are weary of the pressure to choose sides and declare an enemy, *Jesus Outside the Lines* will show you a refreshingly different path.

TROY TOMLINSON
President and CEO of Sony ATV Music Nashville

I used to wonder why my dear friend Scott Sauls wasn't already a published author, for I've learned so much from my younger brother. But I'm glad he waited. *Jesus Outside the Lines* isn't a first book; it's more like fine wine, distilled wisdom, and the vintage aroma of grace. Thank you, Scott, for showing me that Christianity is both true *and* beautiful; that I matter, but that I'm not the point; that the family of God is bigger than my favorite tribe in the family; that contextualizing the gospel isn't compromising the gospel; that God loves the world, not just people in the world; that Jesus isn't nervously pacing the corridors of heaven, he's actively making all things new. Thank you, Scott, for reminding me the gospel is *so much* bigger and better than I can imagine.

SCOTTY SMITH
Founder of Christ Community Church in Franklin, Tennessee, and author of *Everyday Prayers*

We live in a cultural moment that has made it feel almost impossible for Christians to find their voice. We feel silenced, marginalized, and in need of defending ourselves. But this reaction has not helped. Choosing sides in the larger cultural conflicts has only left us feeling misunderstood, stereotyped, and caricatured. We long for another way. And this is what Scott has given us in this book. With theological insight, cultural astuteness, and the compassionate tone of Jesus, he paints a way for the church to have influence without coercion and put the brilliance of Jesus on display in a pluralistic world. A worthy read.

JON TYSON
Founding pastor of Trinity Grace Church, New York, and author of *Sacred Roots: Why the Church Still Matters*

Scott Sauls is my pastor and friend. He is a man who deeply loves Christ. He is not a Christian writer as much as he is a writer and pastor and father and husband and brother and son who is a Christian, a follower of Christ. Scott's words will challenge you, make you mad and happy, make you cry and make you laugh. Art is supposed to make you feel something and glorify God all at the same time. I believe he accomplishes that!

TOM DOUGLAS
Hall of Fame songwriter

As a pastor, it's a given that Scott would comb the Scriptures for answers to so many cultural issues we're facing today; but he also puts his own story and life into each chapter. I'm so thankful for the overall tone of the book, which combines bold, substantive truth with humility and grace. *Jesus Outside the Lines* will be an amazing companion to those of us attempting to be "salt and light" in our world.

LEE NORWOOD
Senior vice president of men's design, Polo Ralph Lauren

The deepest learning we do is always over the shoulder and through the heart. In *Jesus Outside the Lines*, Scott Sauls invites everyone everywhere into an honest conversation about the things that matter most—and therefore at the same time are the most tender and contentious for us. But he does so as a friend, offering thoughtful, rich, even pastoral counsel for believer and unbeliever alike, longing as he does that we find ways to flourish as human beings who have commitments and convictions about God, politics, money, sexuality, and more, agreeing to disagree where we must, but with love and respect, with listening and friendship. In our polarizing world, where the more we know about each other means the less we care for each other, Scott's vision is a gift for those who care for our common good.

STEVEN GARBER
Founder and principal of the Washington Institute for Faith, Vocation & Culture and author of *Visions of Vocation: Common Grace for the Common Good*

I've always valued my conversations and friendship with Scott Sauls, particularly when it comes to his vision of countercultural acts of love, justice, and service. As a QB in the NFL for the past seventeen years, I appreciate Scott putting to paper the feelings and discussions that we often engage in amidst the locker-room setting. Scott boldly and bravely addresses polarizing issues we deal with today in ways I've previously never considered. Thoughtfully reflecting on *Jesus Outside the Lines*, I realize this book paints a clear picture of what I hope to become as a follower of Christ.

MATT HASSELBECK
NFL quarterback

Scott Sauls is a refreshing voice, seasoned with maturity and grace regarding the complex issues of our time. He tackles topics that have long created division with such heartfelt hope that I'm more encouraged than ever about the future of the church.

REBEKAH LYONS
Cofounder of *Q* and author of *Freefall to Fly*

Scott takes on key issues in an honest and candid manner and helps us understand them in a way that is humane, biblical, and ultimately Christlike. I want to care more for my friends, be quicker to listen to others, and yet with more conviction live for the One who truly offers us life in all its fullness. *Jesus Outside the Lines* is a helpful companion for this endeavor.

> **KEITH GETTY**
> Hymn composer

Jesus Outside the Lines is a valuable encouragement in my quest to live with Jesus and follow his command to love my neighbor. Scott Sauls touches on the most relevant issues a follower of Jesus confronts in our present-day culture. He brings clarity and direction for living in a way that promotes Jesus and builds his Kingdom. Scott's thoughts are honest, refreshingly real, and, most of all, helpful to me. I have gained a more insightful understanding of how Jesus' thoughts should affect my own thoughts and how I can live out his commands in my day-to-day walk.

> **BEN CRANE**
> PGA Tour golf professional

In *Jesus Outside the Lines*, Scott Sauls has provided an insightful approach to engaging our world, which is too often fraught with deep-seated conflict and historical divisions. Scott calls us to affirm the dignity of all persons. He urges us to resist the temptation to see each other simply from our own perspective but to see each other as image bearers of God, challenging us to love our neighbors with a radical and honest humility.

> **ELISE CHONG**
> Executive director of Hope for New York

Scott Sauls has written a gem. *Jesus Outside the Lines* is brilliant, accessible, compelling, and compassionate. Scott has his finger on the pulse of a culture that has given up on inadequate representations of Jesus and the Christian faith. With a pastoral tone and apologetic skill, he debunks those misrepresentations and invites us into the joy of faithfully pursuing the biblical Jesus while he equips us to have a better dialogue with those who have yet to encounter him.

> **JR VASSAR**
> Pastor of Church at the Cross and author of *Glory Hunger: God, the Gospel, and Our Quest for Something More*

The kind of voice we increasingly need to help guide deep and respectful conversation around the claims of Jesus is one of humility, kindness, and humor. Judging by this book, Scott Sauls is beginning to emerge as one of our best voices.

SAMMY RHODES
Campus minister, writer, and humorist

In *Jesus Outside the Lines*, my pastor Scott Sauls provides a path for those less interested in "going to church" and more eager to "be the church." He presses us toward a keen awareness of the image of God in humanity, thoughtfully engaging us to love each and every neighbor, not just a select few, even as we love ourselves. Scott calls us to subversive, countercultural acts of love, justice, and service for the common good with a vision to further the Kingdom of God in our time. If you are looking to be an active and life-giving contributor to God's mission, you need to look no further than *Jesus Outside the Lines*.

DANNY HERRON
President/chief executive officer of Habitat for Humanity of Greater Nashville

The "conform or else" mentality of our late modern culture is disheartening, lamentable, and transgressive to human flourishing. Yet the root of the problem isn't "out there" in our culture, but "in here" in our hearts. In *Jesus Outside the Lines*, Scott Sauls is authentic and vulnerable as he wisely and gently reminds us of our brokenness and shows us how the power and beauty of the gospel can heal us, from the inside out.

BETHANY JENKINS
Founder of the Park Forum and director of the Gospel Coalition's "Every Square Inch"

Scott Sauls gives us a compelling vision for how to follow the real Jesus in real life. *Jesus Outside the Lines* is a guide to living in the fullness of God's kingdom here on earth that helps followers of Jesus love both God and the world around them.

DARRIN PATRICK
Author, lead pastor of The Journey Church in St. Louis, Missouri, and vice president of the Acts 29 Network

From disagreements to unity, from outrage to true humility, Scott Sauls's *Jesus Outside the Lines* offers grace as the compelling alternative to the current social norms of judgment and reductionism. Fueled by how Jesus embodied his words and loved his enemies, Scott's book offers a conversational and winsome reminder to be attentive to particulars in a world of generalities. The book is an invitation to respect one another, even when we disagree. When this kind of generosity is the banner, truth and love come together and triumph over tribal divisions.

SANDRA McCRACKEN
Singer/songwriter

I admire Scott Sauls as I admire few other pastors. And now all of us can benefit from him through his writing. *Jesus Outside the Lines* is the message we need to hear right now, as our nation is so deeply divided. Just imagine the peace we could enjoy together if we erased our self-invented lines and let Jesus redraw them for us in his own unsettling, beautiful way. Scott's book can free us to do so.

RAY ORTLUND
Author and lead pastor of Immanuel Church in Nashville, Tennessee

As my former pastor and colleague, and now friend, I have always known Scott Sauls to provide thoughtful and considered perspectives on a wide range of topics and theological tangles. Though I differ in thinking from Scott on some points, I appreciate the way he approaches some of the more controversial issues facing the church and the world in the spirit of Christ and his desire for reconciliation. Scott knows so much about God's grace, and he shares that here in this book. I highly recommend it.

JULIET VEDRAL
Executive editor, *The Wheelhouse Review*

As Christians with strong convictions, we often feel the need to argue and defend our positions. And certainly, we should be prepared to give a reason for the hope we have and to articulate important doctrines. But as Scott explains, we can do so in a winsome way that doesn't alienate or demonize those who disagree with us. We need to seek to understand before seeking to be understood. We need to extend grace and compassion. In short, if we want to change the current antagonistic culture that pervades much of the church, we must learn to love our enemies, not just our tribe. In *Jesus Outside the Lines*, Scott shows us how.

JULIE ROYS
Speaker, blogger, freelance journalist, and host of *Up for Debate*, a national talk program on the Moody Radio Network

In our age of explosion of readable media, I, ironically, find myself reading less and less, unless it is within my immediate field of research interest. As I began reading Scott Sauls's *Jesus Outside the Lines*, however, I knew I was encountering something truly extraordinary. Now that I've finished reading, this would be the very first book I'd recommend to *anyone* who wants to get beyond the incessant cultural and political strife—so prevalent in our time—which inexorably begets the erosion of genuine Christian faith. In fact, I would recommend this to my own child as the first cultural primer as a sojourner on his way to the City of God. *Tolle lege!*

PAUL C. H. LIM
Vanderbilt Divinity School, Nashville, Tennessee

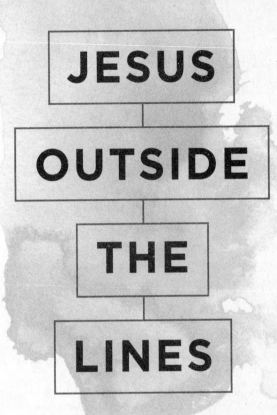

JESUS OUTSIDE THE LINES

*a way forward for those
who are tired of taking sides*

Scott Sauls

Tyndale House Publishers, Inc.
Carol Stream, Illinois

Visit Tyndale online at www.tyndale.com.

Visit the author's website at www.scottsauls.com.

TYNDALE and Tyndale's quill logo are registered trademarks of Tyndale House Publishers, Inc.

Jesus Outside the Lines: A Way Forward for Those Who Are Tired of Taking Sides

Designed by Daniel Farrell

Edited by Jane Vogel

Published in association with the literary agency of Wolgemuth & Associates, Inc.

Library of Congress Cataloging-in-Publication Data

Sauls, Scott.
    Jesus outside the lines : a way forward for those who are tired of taking sides / Scott Sauls.
        pages cm
    Includes bibliographical references.
    ISBN 978-1-4964-0093-2 (sc)
1. Christian life. I. Title.
    BV4501.3.S283 2015
    261—dc23   2014046052

Printed in the United States of America

21   20   19   18   17   16
9   8   7   6   5

TABLE OF CONTENTS

Acknowledgments *xiii*
Foreword by Gabe Lyons *xv*
Introduction: Jesus Outside the Lines *xvii*

Part One: Jesus Outside the Lines of My Christian Tribe

CHAPTER ONE   Red State or Blue State? *3*
CHAPTER TWO   For the Unborn or for the Poor? *21*
CHAPTER THREE   Personal Faith or Institutional Church? *41*
CHAPTER FOUR   Money Guilt or Money Greed? *59*

Part Two: Jesus Outside the Lines of Christianity

CHAPTER FIVE   Affirmation or Critique? *81*
CHAPTER SIX   Accountability or Compassion? *99*
CHAPTER SEVEN   Hypocrite or Work in Progress? *115*
CHAPTER EIGHT   Chastity or Sexual Freedom? *133*
CHAPTER NINE   Hope or Realism? *151*
CHAPTER TEN   Self-Esteem or God-Esteem? *171*
EPILOGUE   Living Outside the Lines *189*

About the Author *199*
Notes *201*

ACKNOWLEDGMENTS

To Wolgemuth & Associates and Tyndale House: thank you for believing in this project enough to partner with me in it.

To friends who gave freely of your time, providing affirming and constructive comments to help make a rough draft less rough—Bo Bartholomew, Bob Bradshaw, Alec Dryden, David Filson, David Flory, Amanda Geisinger, Andy Hill, Michael Keller, Llew Ann King, Chuck Merritt, Stephen Moss, Kaka Ray, Sammy Rhodes, Clay and Amy Richards, Jen Seger, Juliet Vedral, John Walter, and Christine Whitford—thank you! Anderson Spickard, I am especially indebted to you for going the extra mile.

To Tim Keller: it is because of your leadership and vision that I am who I am as a minister.

To the members of Christ Presbyterian Church in Nashville: you are family.

To Abby and Ellie: you are beautiful, special, and loved. Don't ever forget that.

To Patti: you are my best friend and the love of my life. Here's to another twenty years of dancing outside the lines.

FOREWORD

I prefer life *inside* the lines.

Clean, straight, black and white. That's way simpler.

Who wants to live in the *gray*, anyway? Blurred lines breed chaos and confusion. All control feels lost. In the gray we are exposed, our vulnerability and uncertainties put on display. To risk existence in the middle ground requires humility, or more—being misunderstood.

But Christians are supposed to know what they think about everything, right? We are the ones tasked with—commissioned even—to go and tell everyone else what to believe, how to act, and whom to judge. Isn't that, at least in part, what it means to be a Christian?

Unfortunately, generations of Christians have grown to think so. But this perspective couldn't be further from the truth. That is, if the truth is Jesus. Deep down we know there's a better way, but we are unsure how to get there.

Enter Scott Sauls.

As a pastor, New Yorker, Southern gentleman, and caring mentor, Scott is an antidote to our dilemma. His experience spans both the intellectual and the practical. He's a breath of fresh air!

We need that kind of leadership. We each sense the disconnection, misunderstanding, and chaos going on within our churches and communities. Opinions are strong, and the stakes seem high. The public square we share is evolving at rapid speed, and we no longer know how to civilly dialogue when we disagree.

For some, the reaction is to recoil. They build walls, label enemies, and defend traditions. This makes things simple, black and white. But is that really how we ought to approach one another—and the neighbor God has called us to love?

Jesus doesn't call us to simple. He calls us into complexity. The human soul, psyche, mind, and emotions are complicated. And if he calls us to anything, it's to enter into the mess that is day-to-day life alongside broken people in the midst of chaotic circumstances.

Scott walks us through some of the most divisive issues of our day. With a kind, loving, and gentle tone, he carefully aids our thinking while respecting our intellect. He gives us just enough of his own delicate influence to discern a way forward, yet he puts that choice in our hands.

Scott's desire to help *real* people engage *real* problems and find *real* answers catapults this book to the top of the stack for anyone wanting to understand how to better engage a divided world. His call for unity and understanding is not to be mistaken as compromise; rather, it is pastoral encouragement to live faithfully even when it feels we are at odds with others.

By the end of this book, I'm sure you'll feel the way I do about Scott. You will have met a caring and thoughtful leader, one who carries a burden of sincere concern for our world while being a trustworthy and reliable guide. He's not interested in stirring up unhelpful, provocative arguments and banter. But rather, Scott presses into the gray—which is outside the lines, knowing it is only there that we find the heart of Jesus.

Gabe Lyons
Founder of Q and author of *The Next Christians*

Introduction

JESUS OUTSIDE THE LINES

*You can safely assume that you've created God in your own image
when it turns out that God hates all the same people you do.*
—ANNE LAMOTT

I decided to write this book because I am tired.

Tired of taking sides, that is.

Are you?

Are you tired of gossip and negative stereotypes? Are you tired
of labeling and being labeled? Are you tired of political caricatures
and talk-show outrage? Are you tired of opinions being presented
as facts? Are you tired of critiques and condemnations that forgo
listening and relationships? Are you tired of indignant blog posts
and tweets and Facebook posts that take a stand against everyone
but that persuade no one? Are you tired of divisions over silly
and secondary things? Are you tired of racism, classism, sexism,
generationalism, nationalism, denominationalism, doctrinalism,
and all other *isms* that stem from the *ism* that feeds them all: elitism? Are you tired of the glass being half empty? Are you tired
of the endless quest to find something to be mad about? Are you
tired of us against God, us against them, and us against ourselves?

Are you tired of the ways that you, too, have succumbed to
the against-ness of it all?

Political cartoonist and *New York Times* op-ed writer Tim

Kreider, who concedes that his job requires him to be "professionally furious," describes a modern epidemic that he calls "outrage porn":

> So many letters to the editor and comments on the Internet have this . . . tone of thrilled vindication: these are people who have been vigilantly on the lookout for something to be offended by, and found it. . . . Obviously, some part of us loves feeling 1) right and 2) wronged. But outrage is like a lot of other things that feel good but, over time, devour us from the inside out. Except it's even more insidious than most vices because we don't even consciously acknowledge that it's a pleasure. We prefer to think of it as a disagreeable but fundamentally healthy reaction to negative stimuli, like pain or nausea, rather than admit that it's a shameful kick we eagerly indulge again and again. . . . [It is] outrage porn, selected specifically to pander to our impulse to judge and punish, to get us off on righteous indignation.[1]

The commitment to feeling 1) right and 2) wronged is a fairly common phenomenon. But is this a fruitful way for Christians in particular to engage in public conversations about the issues of the day? Jesus taught us a different way.

Tim Keller writes, "Tolerance isn't about not having beliefs. It's about how your beliefs lead you to treat people who disagree with you."[2] This is where biblical Christianity is unparalleled in its beauty and distinctiveness. I am not talking about distorted belief systems that pretend to be Christianity, yet are not. I am talking about the true, pure, undefiled, unfiltered, and altogether biblical and beautiful system of belief—the one that leads people to trust God and have hope for humanity, to visit orphans and widows in their afflictions, to love neighbors who are near and who are in need, and to extend kindness to enemies:

> You have heard that it was said, "Love your neighbor and hate your enemy." But I tell you, love your enemies and pray for those who persecute you, that you may be children of your Father in heaven. He causes his sun to rise on the evil and the good, and sends rain on the righteous and the unrighteous. If you love those who love you, what reward will you get? Are not even the tax collectors doing that? And if you greet only your own people, what are you doing more than others? Do not even pagans do that? Be perfect, therefore, as your heavenly Father is perfect.[3]

Jesus did not merely speak these words as an edict from on high. He *became* these words. "God *shows* his love for us in that while we were still sinners, Christ died for us."[4] While we were running from him, while we were passively resisting him, while we were actively opposing him, while we were his enemies, Christ—compelled by love—died in our stead.

Do we need any more reason than this to extend kindness to those who don't see things as we do? Having received such grace, Christians have a compelling reason to be remarkably gracious, inviting, and endearing toward others, including and especially those who disagree with us. Are we known by what we are for instead of what we are against? Are we less concerned about defending our rights—for Jesus laid down his rights—and more concerned

When the grace of Jesus sinks in, we will be among the least offended and most loving people in the world.

about joining Jesus in his mission of loving people, places, and things to life?

When the grace of Jesus sinks in, we will be among the least offended and most loving people in the world.

Jesus Outside the Lines of My Christian Tribe

Jesus loves the element of surprise. He loves to meet us in places where we least expect him—in places that contradict our assumptions and sensibilities, in places where we are least likely to be looking for him. One of these places is in the lives of other believers with whom we disagree on important, but less-than-essential beliefs.

I am told that the theologian R. C. Sproul once gave a talk at our church—Christ Presbyterian in Nashville, Tennessee—on how God and people come into relationship with one another. On this particular subject, Dr. Sproul is known to emphasize the sovereign, electing grace of God. Others, like Billy Graham, are known to emphasize human free will. While Dr. Sproul would say we choose God only because God first chose us, Dr. Graham would say that God chose us based on his prior knowledge that we would someday choose him. This is an intramural debate between believers. It is an important issue, but it is not a determining factor in anyone's eternal destiny.

During the question-and-answer time after Dr. Sproul's talk, someone asked him if he believed he would see Billy Graham in heaven, to which he replied, "No, I don't believe I will see Billy Graham in heaven." Of course, there was a collective gasp. But then he continued, "Billy Graham will be so close to the throne of God, and I will be so far away from the throne of God, that I will be lucky to even get a glimpse of him!"

R. C. Sproul demonstrated that sincere believers can disagree on certain matters, sometimes quite strongly, and still maintain great respect and affection for one another. What's more, they can find glimpses of Jesus in one another—glimpses that may not be as evident within the confines of their own theological tribes.

The longest recorded prayer we have from Jesus is his famous High Priestly Prayer,[5] in which he asks God that his wildly diverse communion of followers would be united as one. It is no coincidence that the apostle Paul begins most of his letters with the two-part salutation "grace to you"—the standard Greek greeting—and "peace to you"—the standard Jewish greeting. It is no coincidence that he insists that Jews and Greeks, slaves and free people, men and women live together *as one* through Jesus Christ.[6] All three of these pairings represented the deepest forms of relational hostility to the first-century reader. Jews looked down their noses at Greeks, and Greeks despised Jews. Men were dismissive toward women, and women were embittered toward men. Free people saw slaves as subhuman, and slaves resented free people. Paul calls for an end to such divisions because Christians are in many ways a band of opposites who, over time, grow to love one another through the centering, unifying love of Jesus.

> The more we move outside the lines of our own traditions and cultures, the more we will also be moving toward Jesus.

But there is more to unity than the cooling down of hostility. Christians from differing perspectives can *learn* and *mature* as they listen humbly and carefully to one another. I treasure the fact that some of my closest "pastor friends" are from traditions other than my own. Besides being excellent company, these friends are meaningful and necessary for my own development as a minister and as a follower of Jesus.

What's more, I don't know where I would be without the influence of others who see certain nonessentials differently than I do. I need the wisdom, reasoning, and apologetics of C. S. Lewis, though some of his theological beliefs are different from mine. I need the preaching and charisma of Charles Spurgeon, though his view of baptism is different from mine. I need the resurrection vision of N. T. Wright and the theology of Jonathan Edwards, though their views on church government are different from mine. I need the passion and prophetic courage of Martin Luther King Jr., the cultural intelligence of Soong-Chan Rah, and the *Confessions* of St. Augustine, though their ethnicities are different from mine. I need the justice impulse and communal passion of Dietrich Bonhoeffer, though his nationality is different from mine. I need the spiritual thirst and love drive of Brennan Manning and the prophetic wit of G. K. Chesterton, though both are Roman Catholics and I am a Protestant. I need the hymns and personal holiness of John and Charles Wesley, though some of their doctrinal distinctives are different from mine. I need the glorious weakness of Joni Eareckson Tada, the spirituality of Marva Dawn, the trusting perseverance of Elisabeth Elliot, the long-suffering spirit of Amy Carmichael, the transparency of Rebekah Lyons, the thankfulness of Ann Voskamp, the Kingdom vision of Amy Sherman, and the integrity of Patti Sauls, though their gender is different from mine.

As St. Augustine reputedly said, "In nonessentials, liberty." To this we might add, "In nonessentials, open-minded receptivity." We Christians must allow ourselves to be shaped by other believers. The more we move outside the lines of our own traditions and cultures, the more we will also be moving toward Jesus.

Jesus Outside the Lines of Christianity

Jesus makes the audacious claim that he *has* the truth and that he *is* the truth. He declares that anyone who knows and receives the truth is going to be set free. But he goes further than this. In his most famous sermon, Jesus says that any claim or idea—no matter how sincere—that contradicts him or his teaching is false and, if not forsaken, will lead to disastrous consequences:

> Everyone then who hears these words of mine and does them will be like a wise man who built his house on the rock. And the rain fell, and the floods came, and the winds blew and beat on that house, but it did not fall, because it had been founded on the rock. And everyone who hears these words of mine and does not do them will be like a foolish man who built his house on the sand. And the rain fell, and the floods came, and the winds blew and beat against that house, and it fell, and great was the fall of it.[7]

Jesus draws a line in the sand. Whether or not our hearts and minds resonate with, respond to, and surrender to the message of his life, death, burial, and resurrection will determine eternal outcomes for us. Our movement toward him in faith or away from him in unbelief, our saying to him, "Thy will be done" or "My will be done," will indicate whether he has graciously drawn us into his Kingdom or justly left us outside of it. We are either part of his family or not part of his family.

In this sense, as far as Jesus is concerned, everyone will ultimately "take a side."

Yet Jesus gave so much of his time, attention, and love to people who did not side with him. A journey through the Gospels shows that he was especially tender toward people who did not believe in him or follow him.

What does this mean for us today? What does this mean for how we Christians, in particular, should relate to those who do *not* believe as we do?

This excerpt from an essay written by a chaplain at Harvard addresses these questions:

> The divide between Christians and atheists is deep.
> . . . I'm dedicated to bridging that divide—to
> working with . . . atheists, Christians, and people
> of all different beliefs and backgrounds on building
> a more cooperative world. We have a lot of work to
> do. . . . My hope is that these tips can help foster
> better dialogue between Christians and atheists and
> that, together, we can work to see a world in which
> people are able to have honest, challenging, and
> loving conversations across lines of difference.[8]

The Harvard chaplain's name is Chris Stedman.

He is an atheist.

Is it possible for those who believe and those who do not believe in Jesus to disagree with each other on sensitive subjects and still maintain meaningful and even loving friendships with one another? As an atheist, Chris Stedman believes it is possible. As a follower of Jesus, I believe it is not only possible but that it is an essential part of Christian life.

> What matters more to us—that we successfully put others in their place, or that we are known to love well?

In theory this sounds reasonable, but in real life it is difficult. As Dostoyevsky writes in *The Brothers Karamazov*, love in practice is a dreadful thing compared to the love in dreams. In real life, disagreeing about sensitive subjects can reveal pain, sorrow, and complexity. It is with this truth in mind that Christians must navigate the complex and often paradoxical waters of conviction and love.

Is it possible to profoundly disagree with someone and love that person deeply at the same time? Is it possible to hold deep convictions and simultaneously embrace those who reject your deep convictions?

Jesus tells us the answer is yes. And he *shows* us the answer is yes.

Are you familiar with Jesus' encounter with the rich young man? Jesus told the man to sell all of his possessions, give to the poor, and then follow him. The man then turned away from Jesus because he had great wealth. There are two incredibly significant details in this account that we may overlook. First, Jesus looked at the man *and loved him*. Second, the man walked away from Jesus feeling *sad*. Not judged. Not ticked off. Sad. He walked away in the tension of paradox—enslaved by his affluence, yet sensing that by walking away from Jesus he might be forfeiting an even greater, more life-giving form of wealth.[9]

What matters more to us—that we successfully put others in their place, or that we are known to love well? That we win culture wars with carefully constructed arguments and political power plays, or that we win hearts with humility, truth, and love? God have mercy on us if we do not love well because all that matters to us is being right and winning arguments. Truth and love can go together. Truth and love *must* go together.

Peter wrote these words into a climate in which Christians were routinely criticized, marginalized, and persecuted:

> In your hearts honor Christ the Lord as holy, always being prepared to make a defense to anyone who asks you for a reason for the hope that is in you; yet do it with gentleness and respect, having a good conscience, so that, when you are slandered, those who revile your good behavior in Christ may be put to shame.[10]

Slanderers and persecutors put to shame . . . *through gentleness and respect.*

I believe that Dan Cathy has been listening to Peter. Dan Cathy, the president of Chick-fil-A, is a Christian who was thrust into the public eye after answering a reporter's question about his beliefs regarding gay marriage. Cathy, wanting to be true to his understanding of what Scripture says about the issue, stated simply that he believes marriage is designed for a man and a woman. What followed was an organized and highly publicized protest against him, his commitment to the Bible, and his business, which was boycotted by many.

> Truth and love can go together. Truth and love *must* go together.

In response to the boycott, scores of Cathy's supporters rallied for "Chick-fil-A Appreciation Day," buying millions of chicken sandwiches in a show of solidarity—a protest against the protest.

Dan Cathy did not personally affirm or join in the protest against the protest.

Instead, he quietly reached out to one of his strongest critics, gay activist Shane Windmeyer, who eventually shared these words in an essay that he submitted to the *Huffington Post*:

> It is not often that people with deeply held and completely opposing viewpoints actually risk sitting down and listening to one another. We see this failure to listen and learn in our government, in our communities and in our own families. Dan Cathy and I would, together, try to do better than each of us had experienced before.
>
> Never once did Dan or anyone from Chick-fil-A ask for Campus Pride to stop protesting Chick-fil-A. On the contrary, Dan listened intently to our concerns and . . . [he] sought first to understand, not to be understood. . . . Dan and I shared respectful, enduring communication and built trust. His demeanor has always been one of

kindness and openness. . . . Dan expressed regret and genuine sadness when he heard of people being treated unkindly in the name of Chick-fil-A—but he offered no apologies for his genuine beliefs about marriage.[11]

Deep disagreement and no apologies for what he believes.
Love, respect, listening, and friendship.
At the same time.

A Way Forward for Those Who Are Tired of Taking Sides

Are you looking for a way forward in which more bridges are built and fewer are burned? Do you want to express your faith in ways that move beyond stereotypes and that are coherent, beautiful, and true? Do you want to be known for the people, places, and things that you are *for* instead of the people, places, and things that you are against? Do you want to overcome the tension of wanting to be true to your beliefs and engage the culture? Are you ready to move away from polarizing conversations and toward Jesus and your neighbor?

This is our journey.

It's a journey that Jesus invites us to embark upon.

It's a journey outside the lines.

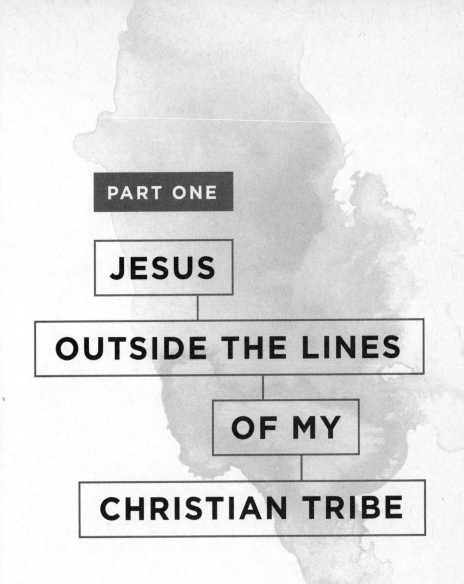

PART ONE

JESUS

OUTSIDE THE LINES

OF MY

CHRISTIAN TRIBE

Chapter One

RED STATE OR BLUE STATE?

I met those of our society who had votes in the ensuing election,
and advised them, 1. To vote, without fee or reward, for the
person they judged most worthy: 2. To speak no evil of the
person they voted against: and, 3. To take care their spirits were
not sharpened against those that voted on the other side.

—JOHN WESLEY

SOMETIMES A SERMON CAN BE A POLARIZING THING. Once I
was preaching to a crowd of New Yorkers about how Christians
should respond to the problem of poverty. I will never forget
two e-mails that I received the following week, both in reference to the same sermon. The writer of the first e-mail, among
other things, accused me of being a right-wing extremist. The
writer of the second e-mail said that he was certain that I must
be a left-wing Marxist.

Time for a career change? I hope not.

There are few subjects that cause people to become more
heated and opinionated than the subject of politics. Yet in the
public discourse, the most heated and opinionated people seem
to get nowhere with their heated opinions. During the 2012
presidential election, a friend of mine posted the following on
his Facebook page:

Dear person passionately pushing your political agenda
on Facebook,

Congratulations! You have convinced me to change my vote. Thank you for helping me see the light.

Appreciatively yours,

No one.

When I received the two critical e-mails in response to my sermon about poverty, I shared them with Tim Keller, who at the time was my boss and mentor. Tim recommended that I seek to learn what I could from the experience, but not to worry too much about the negative feedback, because it could actually be a good sign. For us preachers, Tim said, the longer it takes people to figure out where we stand on politics, in all likelihood the more faithfully we are preaching Jesus.

As is the case with every paradox associated with Christianity, there is a *both/and* and a *neither/nor* component to Christianity as it relates to political loyalties. Unless a human system is fully centered on God (no human system is), Jesus will have things to affirm and things to critique about it. The political left and the political right are no exception.

That helps me. I hope it will help all of us, especially those who are tired of the rancor and caricature that so often accompany political discussions.

The Bible and Government

The first thing I want to say about government is that God is in favor of it. This should encourage anyone with a career in public service. Presidents, members of Congress, governors, mayors, aldermen and alderwomen, as well as police officers, military personnel, park and school district employees, and other public servants play an important role in God's plan to renew the world.

The Bible identifies three institutions that God has established to resist decay in society and promote its flourishing. These are the nuclear family, the church, and the government. The focus of this chapter is to consider specifically what the Bible says about government.

We know that Jesus paid taxes and encouraged his disciples to do the same.[1] To those living in Rome, whose government was not always friendly to Christians, the apostle Paul encouraged submission to the governing authorities, who are "ministers of God" and to whom taxes, respect, and honor are owed. Peter likewise tells believers that part of their service to the common good is to fear God and honor the Roman emperor.[2]

> As is the case with every paradox associated with Christianity, there is a *both/and* and a *neither/nor* component to Christianity as it relates to political loyalties.

The Bible also highlights God-fearing men and women who served in public office. Debra served as judge over Israel, Joseph served as prime minister for the Egyptian pharaoh, Daniel served in the court of Nebuchadnezzar's Babylon, and Nehemiah was a trusted official for the Persian king Artaxerxes. Jesus gave high praise to a Roman soldier for his exemplary faith.[3] These and other examples confirm that government, whether in theocratic ancient Israel or secular Egypt, Babylon, Persia, or Rome, has always been part of God's plan.

Whose Side Is Jesus On?

When it comes to politics, the Bible gives us no reason to believe that Jesus would side completely with one political viewpoint over another. Rather, when it comes to kings and kingdoms, *Jesus sides with himself.*

The following encounter between Joshua, an Israelite military commander headed into battle, and the angel of the Lord is instructive:

> When Joshua was by Jericho, he lifted up his eyes and looked, and behold, a man was standing before him with his drawn sword in his hand. And Joshua went to him and said to him, "Are you for us, or for our adversaries?" And he said, "No; but I am the commander of the army of the LORD. Now I have come." And Joshua fell on his face to the earth and worshiped and said to him, "What does my lord say to his servant?" And the commander of the LORD's army said to Joshua, "Take off your sandals from your feet, for the place where you are standing is holy." And Joshua did so.[4]

Lord, are you for us or for our adversaries? "No, I'm not," he replies.

The question, then, is not whether Jesus is on our side but whether we are on his. This is the appropriate question not only for politics and government but also every other concern.

It may surprise us to know that there was political diversity among Jesus' disciples. Included in the Twelve are Simon, a Zealot, and Matthew, a tax collector. This is significant because Zealots worked *against* the government, while tax collectors worked *for* the government. Interestingly, Matthew the tax collector emphasizes this diversity more than any of the other Gospel writers.[5] Despite their opposing viewpoints, Matthew and Simon were friends, and Matthew wanted us to know this.

Matthew's emphasis on a tax collector and a Zealot living in community suggests a hierarchy of loyalties, especially for Christians. Our loyalty to Jesus and his Kingdom must always exceed our loyalty to an earthly agenda, whether political or otherwise. We should feel "at home" with people who share our faith but not our politics even more than we do with people who share our politics but not our faith. If this is not our experience, then we very well may be rendering to Caesar what belongs to God.

People from varying political persuasions can experience unity under a single, first allegiance to Jesus the King, who on the cross removed and even "killed" the hostility between people on the far left, people on the far right, and people everywhere in between.[6] Wherever the reign of Jesus is felt, differences are embraced and even celebrated as believers move toward one another in unity and peace.

Now let's consider two different ways to look at politics. First, we will consider the world's politics. Then we will look at the politics of God's Kingdom.

The World's Politics

In the eighteenth chapter of John's Gospel, we see a clash between two governors: Pontius Pilate, the governor of Rome, and Jesus Christ, the governor of the universe.[7]

Jesus is brought to Pilate by an angry mob. The mob charges Jesus with being an enemy of the state and a threat to Caesar's preeminence. Pilate, wanting to hear the account directly from Jesus, asks him, "Are you the king of the Jews?" Jesus responds, "You say that I am a king. For this purpose I was born and for this purpose I have come into the world—to bear witness to the truth." Not sensing Jesus to be a threat, Pilate says dismissively to the crowd, "I find no guilt in him."[8] But then he makes a concession according to Jewish custom to release one man for them at the Passover. The crowd pressures Pilate to release Barabbas, a known murderer and insurrectionist, and to crucify

Jesus in Barabbas's place. Wanting to please the crowds, Pilate accommodates. Jesus, the innocent man, gets the death penalty. Barabbas, the guilty man, goes free. Modern politics can also work this way.

The goal of politics is to get people to support a particular vision for the world and to conduct their lives according to that vision. In pursuit of this goal, politicians today often use the same strategies that Jesus' accusers and Pilate employed: misuse of power and manipulation of truth.

The Misuse of Power

The world's politics rely heavily on power. Pilate finds himself caught between a rock and a hard place: he believes that Jesus is innocent; he also knows that Barabbas is guilty. Yet the calculating governor is desperate to please the crowds. As he considers the accusations against Jesus, he goes back and forth between his private chamber and then back out to the crowds. Though he knows who is innocent and who is not, he can't decide whom to crucify and whom to set free.

What is happening here? We can assume that Pilate is taking the temperature of the crowd. He is assessing potential outcomes, discerning which course of action will be best for his own approval rating as well as the preservation of his own stature. His conscience makes him reluctant to crucify Jesus, yet he wants the favor of the crowd. But in worldly politics, when conscience and the crowd are at odds with one another, the crowd always wins. When the crowd always wins, bad people can go free and good people suffer.

I love the animated movie *Shrek* for many reasons. There is so much about the human experience that the film gets right. One such example is the pitiful little ruler of the land, Lord Farquaad.

Farquaad is a single man. The one thing he feels is missing from his kingdom is the lovely princess Fiona, who has long been locked up in a castle far away, guarded by a deadly, fire-breathing dragon. There have been many failed attempts to rescue Fiona; many would-be rescuers have lost their lives.

Farquaad gathers his bravest knights together for a competition. The knights are placed inside an arena to duel against each other until only one of them is left standing. The prevailing knight will have the "honor" of going out on Lord Farquaad's behalf to rescue Fiona. Farquaad, himself a coward, offers the following "inspirational" speech to the knights before they turn against each other in the arena:

> Brave knights, you are the best and brightest in all
> the land. Today one of you shall prove himself. That
> champion shall have the honor—no, no—the privilege
> to go forth and rescue the lovely Princess Fiona from
> the fiery keep of the dragon. If for any reason the
> winner is unsuccessful, the first runner-up will take his
> place and so on and so forth. Some of you may die, but
> it's a sacrifice I am willing to make.[9]

The world's politics. *Your* hopes, desires, ambitions, good name—and, if necessary, your life—are worth sacrificing in order to protect and advance *my* agenda. And I will use my power, the authority of my office, to ensure that this happens. *Some of you may die. But it's a sacrifice I am willing to make.* The ends justify the means.

Manipulation of the Truth

The world's politics are also laced with manipulation of the truth, also known as "spin." We see this in the exchange between Pilate and the accusing crowds. When Pilate asks Jesus if he is king of the Jews, Pilate is not interested in spiritual matters. He wants the answer to one question: *Is this man a threat to my power?* Is he an enemy of Caesar, and therefore also my enemy? What is the size of his following? What is his agenda? What kind of momentum is there behind his movement?

Pilate would not be asking any of these questions about Jesus had the crowds not spun Jesus' teaching on the Kingdom of God to mean that Jesus was an enemy of the state. In reality this is a silly and baseless accusation, because Christ's teaching directs his followers to honor those in authority in every way possible. This being true, to the degree that Christians follow the teachings of Jesus, they will actually be perceived as the most *refreshing and cooperative* citizens of any earthly kingdom.

Pilate's agenda was of no concern to Jesus' accusers, because Jesus' growing influence threatened the status quo for them as well. In order to keep Jesus at bay, they created a false narrative about him and went public with it. Eventually it got him killed.

How about us? Are we also prone to exaggerate, spin, and tell half-truths to protect (or usurp) the status quo? How easy it can be to get pulled in to the politics of spin. Some of us have become so used to these tactics and so numb to them that we— yes, even we who claim to be people of truth—have become willing participants in the spin.

On this side of the aisle is our candidate, the answer to all of the world's problems. She can do no wrong. On that side of the aisle is their candidate, the reason for all of the world's problems. He can do no right.

Are such partisan caricatures and political absolutes a Christian practice, or are they decidedly un-Christian? What do you think?

Leaning toward a certain party is one thing (Matthew did it, Simon did it, and Jesus allowed it), but it is important to see that a partisan spirit can actually run against the Spirit of God. If there ever was a partisan crowd in the Bible, it was the crowd that pressured Pilate to crucify Jesus instead of Barabbas.

Barabbas, a true criminal, went free while Jesus, an innocent man, was executed after having his impeccable character assassinated. This is the essence of partisanship. Partisans inflate the best features of their party while inflating the worst features, real or contrived, of the other party. They ignore the weaknesses of their own party while dismissing the other party's strengths.

I have good friends on both sides of the political aisle. I trust them. Many of them—on both sides—have a strong commitment to their faith. Because of this I grow perplexed when Christian men and women willingly participate in spin—ready, willing, and armed to follow the world in telling half-truths to promote their candidates, while telling more half-truths to demonize their opponents. Have we forgotten that a half-truth is the equivalent of a full lie? What's more, political spin is polarizing even within the community of faith.

A Generational Shift

As a pastor I have been struck by what appears to be a strong reaction among the millennial generation (young adults between the ages of eighteen and thirty-five) toward the faith of their baby boomer parents. Some surveys suggest that millennials are either leaving the church or adopting an altogether different expression of Christianity than the one in which they were raised. In an interview with *Rolling Stone* magazine, reporter Brian Hiatt asked Marcus Mumford whether he still considers himself a Christian. Mumford, a pastor's son and a famous millennial (he is lead singer of the band Mumford & Sons), had this to say:

> I don't really like [the word *Christian*]. It comes with
> so much baggage. So, no, I wouldn't call myself a
> Christian. I think the word just conjures up all these
> religious images that I don't really like. I have my

personal views about the person of Jesus and who he was. . . . I've kind of separated myself from the culture of Christianity.[10]

When those who feel a need to distance themselves from Christianity are asked why, Mumford and other millennials cite several reasons. At the top of the list is weariness over the association of right-wing politics with mainstream Christianity. The "culture of Christianity" that Mumford and others want no part of tends to trace directly back to this association. In the realm of politics, millennials have culture-war fatigue.

With this has come a pendulum swing. Wearied by their parents' right-leaning politics, many millennials have shifted toward the political left. There are good things about this phenomenon. Younger, more progressive-minded believers are bringing a renewed zeal for biblical values such as service, care for the poor, inclusion of people on the margins, ethnic and cultural diversity, and other forms of social justice into their communities. What one wonders, however, is how a generational shift to the political left will play out in the long run. Do millennials risk repeating their parents' errors, the only difference being a co-opting of blue-state sensibilities into faith instead of red-state ones? Will their children sense an imbalance in them as well? Only time will tell.

The Politics of God's Kingdom

Please don't hear me saying that it is wrong for a Christian to support one political party over another. Christians have liberty in things that are nonessential, including politics; that's the point I am trying to make here. The political left and the political right both have good things to say, and both have their problems as well. It can be damaging to think otherwise.

For example, during the 1992 presidential elections a friend of mine told me about an awkward moment in his Bible study. One of the group members expressed excitement because that Sunday, she had seen a bumper sticker promoting the "other party" in the church's parking lot. She was excited because, to her, this was an indication that non-Christians had come to visit. Imagine the awkwardness when another member of the group chimed in, "Um . . . that's my bumper sticker that you saw."

Can we talk? If a Zealot and a tax collector share a common faith that transcends opposing political loyalties, then left-leaning and right-leaning believers must do the same. It is wrong to question someone's faith because they don't vote like you do. Yes, *wrong*.

It's Not about Which Side of the Aisle

More recently, a member of our church asked me if I could help him find a Bible study group filled with people he doesn't agree with politically. This really encouraged me, because it shows that there are indeed some Christians who value the growth and sharpening that can come from diversity, including political diversity. This is a man who, unlike those whose maturing process is stunted by blind partisan loyalty, is on a fast track toward greater maturity. As he opens himself to learn from the perspective of others, he also moves toward Jesus, who is neither conservative nor liberal, yet is also both.

> Jesus is neither conservative nor liberal, yet he is also both.

In many ways, Jesus is more conservative than the far right. For instance, he says that "not an iota, not a dot, will pass from the Law until all is accomplished."[11] He warns that anyone who adds to or takes away from the words of his Book will not share in the tree of life or the Holy City. He emphasizes the importance of evangelism and conversion and said that unless you are born again, you cannot see the Kingdom of God.[12] These are all hallmarks of today's conservative Christians.

Jesus is also in many ways more liberal than the far left. In saying repeatedly, "You have heard that it was said . . . But I say to you . . . ," he upends the long-held traditions of his time, establishing a new vision for the world for anyone who would receive it.[13] In this, Jesus is quite subversive with respect to the cultural norms of his time. He says that traditional Jews and modern Gentiles should not separate, but should stay in community together, and that serving the poor is central to his mission.[14] That's all very progressive of him.

How Do We Know We Are on God's Side?

The politics of God's Kingdom are different from the world's politics. Kingdom politics reject the world's methods of misusing power and manipulating the truth. What does it look like for Christians to live out Jesus' Kingdom vision in our daily lives? It looks like taking care of widows and orphans, advocating for the poor, improving economies, paying taxes, honoring those in authority, loving our neighbors, pursuing excellence at work, and blessing those who persecute us. When this happens, kings, presidents, governors, mayors, law enforcement officers, park officials, and other public servants will take notice. Those in authority will begin to see Christians as an asset to society. They will recognize and appreciate that Christians, as citizens first and foremost of God's Kingdom, value leaving the world in better shape than we found it. Consider these words from C. S. Lewis:

> If you read history you will find that the Christians
> who did the most for the present world were just those
> who thought most of the next. . . . The conversion of

the Roman Empire, the great men who built up the Middle Ages, the English Evangelicals who abolished the Slave Trade, all left their mark on Earth, precisely because their minds were occupied with Heaven. It is since Christians have largely ceased to think of the other world that they have become so ineffective in this.[15]

Let's consider for a moment what history does in fact tell us.

CHRISTIANITY HAS ALWAYS THRIVED MOST AS A LIFE-GIVING MINORITY, NOT A POLITICAL MAJORITY

Some believe that putting Christians in office and other places of power is the key to transforming the world. "If only there were more people in power who followed Jesus," the reasoning goes, "*that* would be the game changer that would finally make the world what God intends it to be." While it is indeed a very good thing for Christians to serve in public office, neither the Bible nor history supports the idea that holding positions of power is *the key* to bringing God's Kingdom to earth as it is in heaven. On this point, Jesus' own resistance to earthly power is telling. At the peak of his popularity, the people wanted him to be king. But he had a different agenda: "Perceiving then that they were about to come and take him by force to make him king, Jesus withdrew again to the mountain by himself."[16]

Why would Jesus resist earthly power? Why would even a "politician" after God's own heart, King David, tell us not to trust in chariots, horses, or princes?[17] Because Christianity always flourishes most as a life-giving minority, not as a powerful majority. It is through subversive, countercultural acts of love, justice, and service for the common good that Christianity has always gained the most ground.

For example, Christians in ancient Rome faced severe opposition and persecution from the state. Yet in this climate, believers had "favor with all the people"[18] because of the refreshing way in which they loved *all* their neighbors. Following many failed attempts to exterminate Christians from Rome, the emperor Julian wrote a letter to his friend Arsacius. In the letter, Julian conceded that the more he tried to destroy Christians, the more their movement grew. Said the emperor, "The impious Galileans [Christians] support not only their own poor but ours as well."[19]

When did Christianity begin to falter in Rome? It began when a later emperor, Constantine, sought to impose Christianity on all of Rome as the state religion. The results were disastrous. Rather than becoming more like the city of God, Rome went into spiritual decline, and the salt of early Christianity eventually lost its savor. The same can be said of many European countries. When those in power made Christianity the state religion, the church began its decline toward irrelevance. More recently, the so-called Moral Majority sought to bring "Christian values" to American society through political activism and "taking a stand" for what they believe. Unfortunately for them, this strategy has had a reverse effect.

CHRISTIANITY EMBRACES BOTH CONSERVATIVE AND PROGRESSIVE VALUES

The Kingdom of Jesus does not advance through spin, political maneuvering, manipulation of power, or "taking a stand" for what we believe (do we ever see Jesus, or for that matter Paul or any of the apostles, taking a stand against secular society or government?). Rather, the Kingdom of Jesus advances through subversive acts of love—acts that flow from conservative *and* progressive values. This is the beauty of the Christian movement. It embraces the very best of both points of view, while pushing back on the flaws, shortcomings, and injustices inherent in both.

How does this work?

By the third century, in spite of a government that stood

against religious freedom (except for the freedom to worship Caesar), the social fabric of Rome had been transformed for the better. Believers in Christ were the chief contributors to this transformation. Here are a few examples:

First, Christians led the way in the movement for women's equality. At that time there were double standards in Rome with respect to gender. A woman was expected to be faithful to her husband, while a man could have multiple mistresses and wives. Unmarried and childless women were ostracized. If a woman's husband died, she had two years to find a new husband before the state would withdraw support and she would likely starve. Christians took up the cause of women, giving them prominent places of honor in the church, taking care of widows as if they were family, and insisting that men be faithful to their wives. In spite of prevailing cultural values, a Christian man was expected to be either single or a "one-woman man," the husband of one wife. The virtue of monogamous sexuality within marriage—a conservative value today—was at play. But so was the progressive virtue of equality—men could no longer treat women as inferior.

> The Kingdom of Jesus advances through subversive acts of love—acts that flow from conservative *and* progressive values.

Second, infanticide was prominent in early Rome. There was no prevailing ethic of life except that certain lives were expendable. Consider this excerpt from a letter by a man named Hilarion to his wife, Alis, who was expecting a child. Hilarion was away on business and sent these instructions about the child in Alis's womb:

Do not worry if when all others return I remain in Alexandria. I beg and beseech of you to take care of the little child, and, as soon as we receive wages, I will send them to you. If—good luck to you!—you have a child, if it is a boy, let it live; if it is a girl, throw it out. You told Aphrodisias to tell me: "Do not forget me." How can I forget you? I beg you therefore not to worry.[20]

It is stunning how upbeat he is toward his wife on the one hand, and how heartless he is toward the child on the other . . . if it is a girl, that is. *"If it is a girl, throw it out."* Sadly, this was all too common in Rome. Christians, however, became known for taking up the cause of orphans (girls, children of other races or with special needs—it didn't matter) by welcoming them into their families and raising them to adulthood. Here we have the conservative virtue of protecting the unborn plus the progressive virtues of championing female equality and social justice.

Third, as in Hitler's Germany, the poor in Rome were coldly viewed as "useless eaters," a drain on society. But in Christian communities the poor were treated with dignity and honor. There was a spirit of compassion and generosity among Christians, which manifested in the sharing of wealth to narrow the income gap—a progressive value. But generosity was voluntary, not forced—a conservative value. I once heard someone say that though the early Christians were monogamous with their bodies, they were promiscuous with their wallets.

My friend Erik Lokkesmoe says that it is the job of Christians to help certain parts of government become unnecessary. Of course he does not mean there should be no government at all, just less need for government in those areas that Scripture entrusts to the church's care. God gave us government to restrain evil and uphold the peace in society. He gave us the church to (among other things) champion the cause of the weak, heal the sick, feed the hungry, and show hospitality to people on the margins. With his statement, Erik calls the church to a renewed vision of being a countercultural movement that works for the good of all.

The Kingdom of God advances on earth as it is in heaven when the people of God, loved and kept by Jesus, assume a public faith that includes, but is certainly not limited to, government. Public faith enriches the world not by grasping for earthly power, but through self-donation. This is how Jesus transformed Jerusalem. This is how Christianity transformed Rome. This is how Christianity can transform any society, including our own.

"Seek first the kingdom of God . . . , and all these things will be added to you."[21]

Chapter Two

FOR THE UNBORN OR
FOR THE POOR?

*The whole concept of the . . . "image of God," is the idea that all men
have something within them that God injected. . . . And this gives
[man] a uniqueness, it gives him worth, it gives him dignity. And we
must never forget this . . . there are no gradations in the image of God.
Every man from a treble white to a bass black is significant on God's
keyboard, precisely because every man is made in the image of God. One
day we will learn that. We will know one day that God made us to live
together as brothers and to respect the dignity and worth of every man.*
—MARTIN LUTHER KING JR.

ONE OF MODERN SOCIETY'S MOST HEATED, polarizing conversations centers on the value of human life. Everyone, of course, will say that they believe human life is sacred. But not everyone seems to treat *all* human life as *equally* sacred.

For example, the political right has historically placed a high value on the sanctity of human life in the womb. The historic *Roe v. Wade* decision, viewed by many as one of the darkest, most tragic verdicts ever handed down by the Supreme Court, has since led to nearly sixty million abortions in the United States. These staggering numbers are unconscionable to those who call themselves "pro-life," many of whom have dedicated time, energy, and money in efforts to overturn *Roe v. Wade* in defense of the unborn. Many of these men and women would say that they are driven by a God-given passion to defend and protect "the least of these," and that it is society's moral obligation to stand with the weak because they are unable to speak for or defend themselves. For Christians on the political right, the pro-life position is so intertwined with the biblical teaching that human life begins at conception[1] that some have been so bold as to proclaim that a vote for the Democratic party is the equivalent of a vote against Jesus.

Similarly, the political left has historically placed a high value on the sanctity of human life outside the womb. Generally speaking, the liberal or progressive wing is known for championing the rights of the postnatal poor, weak, and oppressed. Many of these men and women also would say that they are driven by a God-given passion to defend and protect "the least of these," and that it is society's moral obligation to stand with the weak because they are unable to speak for or defend themselves. For Christians on the political left, the pro-poor and weak and oppressed position is so intertwined with the biblical teaching that Jesus, too, is for the poor and weak and oppressed[2] that some have been so bold as to proclaim that a vote for the Republican party is the equivalent of a vote against Jesus.

> "Truly, I say to you, as you did it to one of the least of these my brothers, you did it to me" (Matthew 25:40).

Responding to conservative concerns related to the unborn, liberals will cry, "What about the mother's health? What about the mother's right to choose what she does with her own body? You anti-choice people show no sympathy or concern for anyone but the fetus!" Conservatives will reply, "You pro-choice people are not pro-choice at all. You are pro-death! What about the child in the womb who isn't given a choice? What about the rights and the health of the weakest and most vulnerable human being in the equation, the one whose rights are taken away by people who don't care about anybody but themselves?"

Responding to the liberal concerns related to the postnatal poor, weak, and oppressed, conservatives will cry, "But we *do* care about the poor and weak and oppressed! If government would get out of the way and allow the private sector to create more jobs and more opportunities, everyone will have a better chance to succeed. Plus, so many people are poor because of their own doing. They are lazy, unmotivated, and unwilling to go out and get a job." Liberals will reply, "If a poor person came to you for an interview, would you hire them? Have you ever interviewed a poor person? Have you ever *met* a poor person? Of course you haven't, because you only pretend to care for the poor. All you really care about is your bottom line!"

And so it goes. Both sides claim that they are upholding the sanctity of human life. Both sides claim that their utmost concern is for "the least of these." Both sides believe without a doubt that Jesus is on their side. And both sides, believing that they possess the moral high ground, launch verbal and digital grenades at the other for having such a low regard for human dignity.

Could it be that both sides are right and both sides are wrong?

Could it be that both sides are lopsided in their emphasis?

Could it be that both sides are prone to privilege one type of human being while dismissing another type of human being?

For Jesus, just as was the case for Martin Luther King Jr., "There are no gradations in the image of God." In other words, in Jesus' eyes there is no such thing as one type of person who is more special than another type of person. A crying infant is as significant and valuable as a famous actor, a homeless person as a president, a student as a teacher, a private as a general, a concessions worker as a quarterback, a patient as a surgeon, and a janitor as a CEO.

Made in God's Image

According to Jesus, every single person ever born is a carrier of the divine imprint. To be human is to be created in the image of God.[3] To be human, therefore, is to be crowned by the Creator with glory and honor:

> O LORD, our Lord,
>> how majestic is your name in all the earth!
> You have set your glory above the heavens. . . .
> When I look at your heavens, the work of your fingers,
>> the moon and the stars, which you have set in place,
> what is man that you are mindful of him,
>> and the son of man that you care for him?
> Yet you have made him a little lower than the heavenly
>> beings
>> and crowned him with glory and honor.[4]

Someone once asked Jesus what the greatest commandment is. Jesus replied that the greatest commandment is to love God with everything you are, and to love your neighbor as yourself. When Jesus was asked, "Who is my neighbor?" he responded with a story about a Samaritan—the most unsavory example he could think of in the eyes of his Jewish audience—who demonstrated the true essence of neighborly love. Your neighbor, according to Jesus, is anyone who is near and anyone who is in need, regardless of gender, race, sexual orientation, economic bracket, politics, culture, or creed. Your neighbor, according to Jesus, is every other human being.

It is an awareness of the image of God in every person—not merely some—that will enable us to love our neighbors as ourselves. Embracing every person's God-given dignity also enables us to declare a cease and desist on a posture that is prone to taking sides and looking for something or someone to be offended by.

The Image of God in You

In the Creation account in Genesis 1–2, we are presented with a brief summary of each creation day. God makes something (land, water, plants, animals, fish, sky, etc.) and then he looks at it and says, "It is good." But after day six, having created the man and the woman, God looks at what he has made and says, "It is *very* good." He saves the superlative statement for the end, as if to say that as magnificent as the universe may be, there is nothing in all Creation that is nearly as magnificent as a human being.

Nashville, Tennessee, became our home three years ago, and it is one of the most beautiful places I have ever seen. There are lovely parks, creeks, trees, rolling hills, and wildlife everywhere. All I need to do is look out our front window to see that yes, the heavens do indeed declare the glory of God. As if this weren't enough, Nashville is also home to many creative people. So much beauty is produced here through the arts—music, film, fashion, theater, etc.—that the city is an aesthetically oriented person's dream come true. If you want to get a glimpse of beauty, come and visit Nashville.

However, it is easy to forget that, according to Jesus, neither nature nor created things represent what is *most* beautiful about Nashville or any other place. The *most* beautiful thing in the world, according to Jesus, is people.

It is people, even more than places and things, who manifest the glory and beauty and magnificence of God. We are made in his image. We are created in his likeness. We are carriers of his imprint.

Ever since they were little, I have pronounced a specific blessing over each of our daughters as I have tucked them into bed at night. The blessing usually starts with a promise or declaration of their human dignity and value straight out of the Bible—"You are fearfully and wonderfully made.[5] . . . Nothing can separate you from the love of God.[6] . . . God will not harm you, but will give you a hope and a future.[7] . . . God so loved you that he gave his only Son for you."[8] The blessing concludes every time with the words, "God made you beautiful and special, and he loves you so much. And so does your daddy. Don't you ever forget that. Amen."

The reason I pronounce this nightly blessing over our daughters is that their hearts, like all human hearts, are prone to forget their fundamental identities as image bearers. I want the last thing they hear before they nod off to be a reaffirmation of what is true. I want them to hear a counter-voice to the shame triggers of our culture and the negative verdicts from within that try to convince them that they are worth less than they actually are. In short, I want them to remember and rest in what God says is true about them. Neither the culture nor their own hearts get to name them, because their Maker already has.

> By this we shall know that we are of the truth and
> reassure our heart before him; for whenever our heart
> condemns us, God is greater than our heart, and
> he knows everything. Beloved, if our heart does not
> condemn us, we have confidence before God.[9]

It is true that all human glory is derivative. We get it from somewhere else, not from within ourselves. But that does not mean that our glory is any less glorious. Just as the moon is made glorious by the light of the sun reflecting off it, we, too, are made glorious as the light of God's beauty shines first upon us, and then through us and off us.

> God, who said, "Let light shine out of darkness," has
> shone in our hearts to give the light of the knowledge
> of the glory of God in the face of Jesus Christ.[10]

And the more the light of God shines in us and through us as we behold the face of Christ, the more like Christ we will become. The more like Christ we become, the more his fractured image in us will be restored. The more his fractured image in us is restored, the less we will want to medicate our fractured egos by putting others down and diminishing others' dignity through gossip, slander, prejudice, and exclusion. And the less we diminish others' dignity, the more we will want to uphold and affirm and celebrate others' dignity as Jesus does. And the more we uphold and affirm and celebrate others' dignity as Jesus does, the less prone we will be to take sides in ways that Jesus does not.

The Image of God in "the Other"

Once we begin to receive Jesus' pronouncement over us, that indeed we are carriers of the divine imprint and crowned with glory and honor and filled with dignity by virtue of the fact that we are human, our perspective toward others will also undergo a transformation.

> **The more we uphold and affirm and celebrate others' dignity as Jesus does, the less prone we will be to take sides in ways that Jesus does not.**

If the divine pronouncement "very good" is true of us because we are made in God's image, it must also be true of others.

> You have heard that it was said, "You shall love your
> neighbor and hate your enemy." But I say to you, Love
> your enemies and pray for those who persecute you, so

that you may be sons of your Father who is in heaven.
For he makes his sun rise on the evil and on the good,
and sends rain on the just and on the unjust. For if you
love those who love you, what reward do you have?
Do not even the tax collectors do the same? And if
you greet only your brothers, what more are you doing
than others?[11]

Did Jesus really mean this? Yes, he did.

We are not only to love those who are like us. We are even—
no, especially—to love those who are not like us. This, in fact,
is the true measure of whether love resides in the heart. This is
the true measure that the light that shines out of darkness is also
shining in and through us.

C. S. Lewis puts this all in perspective in his brilliant essay
"The Weight of Glory":

It is a serious thing to live in a society of possible gods
and goddesses, to remember that the dullest and most
uninteresting person you can talk to may one day be a
creature which, if you saw it now, you would be strongly
tempted to worship, or else a horror and a corruption
such as you now meet, if at all, only in a nightmare.
All day long we are, in some degree, helping each
other to one or other of these destinations. It is in the
light of these overwhelming possibilities, it is with the
awe and the circumspection proper to them, that we
should conduct all of our dealings with one another, all
friendships, all loves, all play, all politics. There are no
ordinary people. You have never talked to a mere mortal.
Nations, cultures, arts, civilisations—these are mortal,
and their life is to ours as the life of a gnat. But it is
immortals whom we joke with, work with, marry, snub,

and exploit—immortal horrors or everlasting splendors.
. . . Next to the Blessed Sacrament itself, your neighbor is
the holiest object presented to your senses.[12]

The holiest object presented to your senses.
There are no ordinary people.

A Comprehensive Ethic of Life

Jesus went out of his way to affirm the dignity of every type of
person. The way that he came into the world and lived his life
is proof positive of this. Though he was God, he did not come
into the world in royalty and opulence. Instead, he chose to be
born in a poor, obscure, small town called Nazareth. His mom
and dad were a couple of newlyweds who didn't know which
end was up. They had zero money, zero connections, and zero
influence in society. Jesus lived a good part of his adult life as
a homeless man, literally having no place to lay his head. The
physical description we have of him tells us that he was not sexy
or "hot." He would not have made it onto the cover of *GQ*.
Truth be told, his physical appearance was, well, homely:

He had no form or majesty that we should look at him,
  and no beauty that we should desire him.
He was despised and rejected by men . . .
and as one from whom men hide their faces
  he was despised, and we esteemed him not.[13]

Jesus' chosen associations were also remarkable, if for no
other reason than that they were all over the place. Jesus became
a friend to all sorts of people. His friends included wealthy
elites, such as Nicodemus and Joseph of Arimathea, and
powerful people, such as the Roman centurion. But he also

reached out in friendship to the culturally despised Samaritan woman at the well and the woman who had been caught in adultery. He reached out to Saul of Tarsus, who, having been trained not only in the Jewish synagogues but also in the Greek classics, possessed the equivalent of an Ivy League degree. But he also reached out to Simon Peter, a common fisherman. In a world where slaves were treated as inferior, Jesus put his hand on a Roman centurion's slave to heal him. In a world where sick people were quarantined and declared to be cursed, Jesus drew near to paralytics, hemophiliacs, the visually impaired, and lepers. He touched them, and he healed them. In a world where the poor were ignored, cast aside, and left to die, Jesus gave special attention to the poor and called them blessed. In a world where women had no rights and no standing, Jesus received women as his disciples and chose women to witness and "evangelize" his resurrection to a room filled with men.

To Jesus, everybody mattered.

While Jesus affirmed the dignity of every type of person, there were two particular types to whom he gave special attention and for whom he had a glaring soft spot. Although society had little time for either group, Jesus went out of his way to communicate to the world how important they were. These were, to a political conservative's delight, little children and, to a political liberal's delight, the poor.

The Dignity of All Children

One day when Jesus was teaching people about the Kingdom of God, some people brought their babies to him to see if he would be willing to touch them. The disciples rebuked the parents for doing so. *Do you know who Jesus is? He is a king, we tell you, the Christ, the Son of the Living God, and the teacher of Israel. Don't you realize that someone of his stature does not have time for children? Don't you realize that he is much more important than this? Do you really think he has time for these messy little noisemakers?*

Jesus rebuked his disciples for this.

Then, he called the children to him, saying, "Let the children come to me, and do not hinder them, for to such belongs the kingdom of God. Truly, I say to you, whoever does not receive the kingdom of God like a child shall not enter it."[14]

Children do not bother Jesus. They are not nuisances to him, and they should not be to us. In fact, they are our very best teachers when it comes to living authentically in the Kingdom of God. It is their raw honesty and dependence and quickness to run to their parents that show us, more than anything else, how God wants us to relate to him. Children, as far as Jesus is concerned, should be both seen and heard.

A few years ago, my friend Gabe Lyons published a moving piece in the *Huffington Post* about his oldest son, Cade. He said the following:

People with Down syndrome have been targeted for extinction. In November, the *New York Post* heralded "The End of Down Syndrome" and profiled a new, safer test for pre-natal detection. Before this test was available, 92 percent of Down syndrome diagnoses (and many times false diagnoses) resulted in the mothers choosing to terminate their pregnancies. With these new tests, some experts foretell the end of Downs.

Why the rush to rid the world of people like Cade?

Certainly, it isn't because his disability physically threatens anyone. Rather, Down syndrome children pose a different kind of threat to society—the in-your-face reminder that our aspirations for "perfection" may be flawed. People like Cade disrupt normal. Whether it's his insistence that everyone he says "hello" to on the busy streets of Manhattan respond in-kind or his unfiltered ability to hug a lonely, wheelchair-bound, homeless man without hesitation: people like Cade bring new dimension to what normal ought to be. . . .

Cade's life, and those like his, offer *an alternative view of the good life.*

These individuals alter career paths and require families to work together. They invite each of us to engage, instead of simply walking by. They love unconditionally. . . . They celebrate the little things in life, and displace the stress that bogs most of us down. They seem to understand what true life is about, more than many of us. They offer us the opportunity to truly value all people as created equal.[15]

I am grateful for Gabe's perspective on Cade, as well as for my own church community, which is dedicated to supporting and affirming people with special needs. There is something so right and so good about this. For it is Jesus who says of the little people, the messy people, the simple people, and the people with special needs, "Let them come, and do not hinder them."

We need Cade and others with his gifts to show us what it looks like to live with special needs.

Because we all have special needs.

And yet *people with Down syndrome have been targeted for extinction.*

This is tragic.

Historically, Christianity has always embraced, affirmed, and sought to protect the lives of unborn children—no matter their condition. Having been fearfully and wonderfully made and knit together by God in their mothers' wombs, all children possess the inalienable right to nurture, nourishment, protection, and advocacy. This is a matter of justice. Jesus is eager to speak on behalf of all kinds of people, but especially those who are not able to speak for themselves.

The degree to which we lose this perspective about the little people among us, the degree to which we decide which categories of humans get to live and which categories do not, is the degree to which we have exchanged the dignity of all humans for Darwin's natural selection theory applied to the human race. The survival of the fittest. Only the strong and preferred get to survive. The strong conquer the weak, who, as the psychopath Adolf Hitler saw it, were nothing but "useless eaters."

When we reduce a human being's right to live all the way down to a cost-benefit analysis and decide to discard the lives that seem to cost more than they contribute, what will be next? This prevailing philosophy about human life will, over time, present even more grotesque injustice than what we have seen thus far.

A few years ago Peter Singer, an atheist and professor of bioethics at Princeton University, said what many were thinking about abortion. *If infanticide inside the womb is legal, then there is no logical reason why infanticide outside the womb should not be legal as well.* If a physician recommends termination of a child inside the womb, what should stop the same physician from recommending a postnatal termination if the child is found to be undesirable?

Upholding the dignity of Cade Lyons is the only way to be consistent in upholding the dignity of anybody. Otherwise Peter Singer is right. Because as soon as we decide that *one* form of human life is disposable, we have lost all ability to defend human rights for *any* form of human life. If we believe an unborn child with Down syndrome should be eliminated because going through with the pregnancy could mean a harder life for the family or for the child, if we believe that such a child would become a drain on the family or on society, then let's at least be consistent. If we were to say these sorts of things about an unborn child then, as Peter Singer said, we would have to say the same about a child who *has* been born but has a disease, or a difficult personality, or undesirable facial features, or the wrong gender. Furthermore, and to be consistent, we would need to do something about those who are physically weak, have a mental illness, are poor, or are elderly.

Can you imagine the world without all these people? Can you imagine what the world would be like if we allowed Hitler (or anyone else) to decide which people are useful and which ones are not? Like Gabe Lyons, my life is so much richer and fuller because of the people with special needs who are in it. Because I, too, have special needs. We all experience brokenness and cope with need. We all need to see how the power of God is made perfect through weakness.

> Not many of you were wise according to worldly
> standards, not many were powerful, not many were
> of noble birth. But God chose what is foolish in the
> world to shame the wise; God chose what is weak in
> the world to shame the strong; God chose what is low
> and despised in the world . . . so that no human being
> might boast in the presence of God. . . . As it is written,
> "Let the one who boasts, boast in the Lord."[16]

"Let the children come to me, and do not hinder them, for to such belongs the kingdom of God."

The Dignity of the Poor

Perhaps there is no greater way for Jesus to uphold the dignity of the poor than by choosing to be poor himself. He was born to an unwed pregnant teenager who was engaged to a humble woodworker. On the night of his birth, there was no place for them to stay, "no room at the inn," so his first introduction to the world was a stable, and his first bed was a trough out of which the farm animals ate.

As an adult, there were times when Jesus had no place to lay his head. Once, he voluntarily went forty days without eating. He spent his last hours on a trash heap, where he finally died between two crooks. Though he was rich, he became poor, so that through his poverty we might become rich.[17]

Besides choosing to be poor himself, Jesus upheld the dignity of the poor and gave special attention to those who had nothing. In his first recorded public sermon, Jesus chose a text from Isaiah, which reads:

> The Spirit of the Lord is upon me,
>> because he has anointed me
>> to proclaim good news to the poor.
> He has sent me to proclaim liberty to the captives
>> and recovering of sight to the blind,
>> to set at liberty those who are oppressed,
> to proclaim the year of the Lord's favor.[18]

Referring to himself, Jesus proceeded to tell his listeners, "Today this Scripture has been fulfilled in your hearing."[19]

Whenever public figures give an inaugural speech, they will make sure that the speech emphasizes the agenda items that are most important and central to their future administrations. Jesus could not have been more clear in *his* inaugural speech about what would be central to *his* agenda. He was going to preach good news to the poor, set captives free, and liberate the oppressed.

Jesus went on to refer to himself as a physician and healer, and he spoke of Naaman the Syrian, a leper who had been cleansed in the days of the prophets.

But his listeners weren't sick. And to them, lepers were cursed beings. Throwaways. Useless eaters. These religious men listening to Jesus preach did not understand. They were not sick or desperately poor. What was Jesus' agenda all about? Their desire was not for cultural underdogs to be liberated, but rather for their privileged establishment to remain the privileged establishment. Their desire was to keep themselves clean from all the messiness involved in moving toward the sick, the poor, and those on the margins. Their desire was to keep themselves free from the costs and inconveniences of love.

After Jesus finished saying these things, the people in the synagogue were enraged. Then they drove him out of the Temple and tried to throw him off a cliff.

How could they be so blind? How could they be so callous to the poor, to the hurting?

How could *we*?

One day when I was living in New York City, I was walking down Broadway and minding my own business when a woman outside a bagel shop asked me if I would buy her something to eat. She was a familiar face in our neighborhood, because she lived outdoors most of the time. She was homeless. Like Jesus, she had no place to lay her head.

Desiring to help her, I offered to buy her a bagel and a coffee. She responded that the coffee would be nice but she would prefer a container of egg salad instead of a bagel. I smiled and said, "Sure, that's no problem."

But I wasn't smiling inside, because to me her request *was* a problem.

I was going out of my way to help her, and she was being picky. Furthermore, a part of me thought she should be grateful for whatever I chose to give her. A bagel cost seventy-five cents. A container of egg salad cost six dollars.

I still remember my own internal dialogue as I went in the shop to purchase the coffee and egg salad for the woman.

Irritated by her request, I cynically fantasized about what I might say to her if I were less polite and did not have a filter. I thought to myself, *Can I also get you some caviar with that?*

Thank God I didn't say anything so coldhearted.

As I handed the woman her coffee and egg salad, she apologized to me for the egg salad request. She told me that softer foods are the only kinds of food that she is able to eat because to chew on anything, especially a bagel, was excruciatingly painful for her diseased teeth and gums.

God have mercy on me for being so callous and critical toward a woman in whose shoes I have never had to walk and whose life I could not begin to understand. Something tells me, Jesus, that maybe I would have been one of the people wanting to throw you over the cliff.

Maybe in that sidewalk conversation it was I, not the woman, who was truly poor.

Privileged people can have a hard time sympathizing with those who have no idea what it feels like to be privileged. We can be incredibly naive about the plight of the poor and the unique pressures that the poor encounter every single day. For example, I recently heard a report that said 60 percent of abortions in America involve a mother who lives below the poverty line. Usually, the father has disappeared from the picture as well.

Poor conditions often breed poor choices.

Most poor people cannot control their conditions.

My friend Darrin Patrick, lead pastor of The Journey church in St. Louis, Missouri, and a lover of baseball (Darrin also serves as a chaplain to the St. Louis Cardinals), once said that it's naive to give yourself credit for hitting a triple if you were born on third base. He also said that it is equally naive to expect a person who was born in the parking lot to get to third base without your help.

Darrin was not trying to raise guilt by making this statement. Instead, he was trying to raise awareness. The conditions in which the poor must live, including the shortage of resources and opportunities to improve their situations, are what make them poor and keep them poor. Because of this, those who are poor and living on the margins *need* others who have resources to partner with effective organizations and efforts[20] that are devoted to the vision of Deuteronomy 15:

> If among you, one of your brothers should become
> poor, in any of your towns . . . you shall not harden
> your heart or shut your hand against your poor brother,
> but you shall open your hand to him and lend him
> sufficient for his need. . . . You shall give to him freely,
> and your heart shall not be grudging when you give
> to him. . . . You shall open wide your hand to your
> brother, to the needy and to the poor, in your land.[21]

When this kind of openhandedness occurs, it will be the giver who receives an even greater blessing than the receiver, because according to Jesus, "it is more blessed to give than to receive."[22]

Why is it more blessed to give? Because God is by nature a giver, and every person carries his imprint and is made in his likeness. God "so loved . . . that he gave."[23] Just like a fish needs water to flourish, so we who are made in God's image need generous hearts and open hands. We have been made to move toward those around us and to respond to others' needs.

Maybe another reason why Jesus says the giver is more blessed is because the giving experience puts the giver in contact with the receiver. My encounter on the street with the woman who wanted egg salad was life altering for me. I walked away from that short conversation reminded that though my teeth and gums are intact (at least for now), there is much about me—namely, in that moment, my calloused heart—that is rotten, damaged, hurting, and in need of the costly soft food of the Lord's bread and the costly sweet drink of the Lord's cup.

My encounter with the woman on Broadway also reminded me of a hymn that I often sing, but sometimes fail to internalize:

Come, ye sinners, poor and wretched,
Weak and wounded, sick and sore;
Jesus, ready, stands to save you,
Full of pity, joined with power.
He is able, he is able;
He is willing; doubt no more. . . .
Let not conscience make you linger,
Nor of fitness fondly dream;
All the fitness he requires
Is to feel your need of him.[24]

The Dignity of All

Rather than invite shame, the sting of being brought face to face with my own hardened, prejudiced, elitist heart invites me back to my center.

Compared to messy little babies, I am not special.

Compared to the hungry woman on Broadway with hurting teeth, I am not special.

But before the face of God, in whose image I am made, I am special. Not more special than the least of these, but special nonetheless. Crowned with glory and honor by the one who lives in unapproachable light. Declared "very good" by the one who is the essence of goodness. Given dignity by a royal king as he pronounces his nightly blessing over me, "I made you beautiful and special and I love you so much. Don't you ever forget that."

My callous, easily irritated heart can find rest in the shadow of his merciful wings. Through Jesus and in Jesus and because of Jesus, I am many things. But useless is not one of them.

In his human relationships, Jesus resists the "survival of the fittest" theory. Instead, he looks past our weaknesses and sees sparks of God's image that he intends, over time, to transform into light so luminous that it shines brighter than the sun.

From the cross where Jesus, the pure image of God, was deconstructed and dismantled, Jesus secured the reconstruction of God's image in us. Now Jesus, the resurrected and returning King, sees the ruins in us and envisions a conduit for God's glory and wholeness. For the crook in us, he envisions a conduit for God's generosity. For the prostitute in us, he envisions a conduit for God's purity and a pure bride for himself. For the coward in us, he envisions a conduit for God's courage and strength. For the violence and rage in us, he envisions a conduit for God's reconciliation and peace. For the struggler and the sufferer in us, he envisions a conduit for God's joy. For the messy baby in us, he envisions a conduit for God's Kingdom vision. For the poor woman in us with hurting teeth, he envisions a conduit for God's compassionate, healing touch.

> Let not conscience make you linger,
> Nor of fitness fondly dream.
> All the fitness he requires
> Is to feel your need of him.

Chapter Three

PERSONAL FAITH OR INSTITUTIONAL CHURCH?

We have been so soaked in the individualism of modern Western culture that we feel threatened by the idea of our primary identity being that of the family we belong to—especially when the family in question is so large, stretching across space and time. The church isn't simply a collection of isolated individuals, all following their own pathways of spiritual growth without much reference to one another. It may sometimes look like that, and even feel like that. And it's gloriously true that each of us is called to respond to God's call at a personal level. You can hide in the shadows at the back of the church for a while, but sooner or later you have to decide whether this is for you or not.

—N. T. WRIGHT

RECENTLY A MAN ASKED ME if I thought it was important for Christians to be part of a local church. As the pastor of a local church, I found his question refreshingly honest.

Before I responded, I asked the man to give me some context for his question. He said that he had not been part of a local church or attended a worship service for quite some time, and he had become quite satisfied with the church alternative that he had created for himself. Rather than wasting his time with what he called "institutionalized religion," he had crafted a Christian experience that was custom-made specifically *for him*. He listened only to music that he liked, downloaded sermons from the Internet by his favorite preachers, read Christian books that interested him, and was part of an informal community of "like-minded believers." They were not part of a local church but got together twice a month to talk about spiritual things. He listed several reasons why he preferred this alternative way of "doing church." He had his Sundays completely free, he never had to sit through boring services, and his charitable giving went only to causes that he believed in. Best of all, he didn't have to deal with bothersome people, unwanted conversations, or church drama.

This man represents what many recognize as a trend in Western society, especially among younger generations. Researcher George Barna, who refers to this group of churchless believers as "revolutionaries," describes their mind-set as follows:

> A common misconception about revolutionaries is that they are disengaging from God when they leave a local church. We found that while some people leave the local church and fall away from God altogether, there is a much larger segment of Americans who are currently leaving churches precisely because they want *more* of God in their life but cannot get what they need from a local church. They have decided to get serious about their faith by piecing together a more robust faith experience.[1]

I appreciate Barna's carefulness to emphasize that many who are leaving the local church are doing so out of frustration rather than rebellion. The fact that these believers are leaving indicates that, at least for a season, they have made an effort to be part of a local church community. They have left not to *get away from* God but in search of a richer, more authentic *experience of* God that for some reason they have been unable to find within the institutional church.

Over the years I have met many others like this. Their feedback about the local church is strikingly consistent, and their disenchantment is often legitimate. Instead of "going to church," they are eager to *be* the church. Instead of being a face in the crowd, they are eager to be a known and needed member of a community. Instead of being passive observers of an event, they are eager to be active contributors to a shared mission. Instead of listening to a preacher pontificate and tell stories from behind a podium, they are eager to be welcomed into a Story that is bigger than the preacher. Instead of sitting in a room full of people who "accept" Jesus but who also seem bored with him, they are eager to find others like them who truly *love* Jesus and who come alive at the mention of his name. Instead of busying themselves with church programs, they are eager to be part of a movement that resembles the book of Acts, where believers kept peripheral things on the periphery and devoted themselves to the main things, such as worshiping God, studying the Scriptures, living in fellowship, breaking bread together, praying together, opening their homes, giving generously to those who had need, and living in such a way that the watching world took notice and the Lord added daily to their number.[2]

So then, instead of rushing straight into a critique of Christians who have decided that they are done with church, some self-reflection is in order for those of us who are still in the church. Since I am a pastor, "revolutionary" critiques of the modern church invite me to carefully evaluate my own ministry context. They invite me to ask the questions that must be asked by a shepherd of God's people and a champion of God's mission in the world. *As a church*, are we living out the biblical vision for worship, community, and mission? And where we are not, are we making our best attempt at moving toward that biblical vision? If not, in some ways it becomes difficult to argue against the "revolutionary" critique. Those of us who are concerned about the "churchless Christian" phenomenon (and I do count myself among the concerned) must first look at ourselves and ask to what degree *we* have contributed to the conditions that tempt some to hit eject on the local church.

The "revolutionary" phenomenon is not a fringe movement.

The number of Christians opting out of church is on the rise. This number includes some well-known and influential Christians, such as Donald Miller, author of *Blue Like Jazz* and other books that speak meaningfully to younger believers. In February of 2014, Miller shared candidly on his blog that he does not attend church very often. He explained that he struggles to connect with God through listening to sermons or singing songs. Instead, Miller meets with God through his work. "I literally feel an intimacy with God when I build my company," he writes. "So, do I attend church? Not often, to be honest. . . . But I also believe the church is all around us, not to be confined by a specific tribe. . . . I worship God every day through my work. It's a blast."[3]

Miller is not alone in his belief that vibrant Christianity can be found outside the local church. Another "revolutionary" Christian is Kelly Bean, author of *How to Be a Christian without Going to Church: The Unofficial Guide to Alternative Forms of Christian Community*. She writes:

> Here I am on a bright Sunday morning, curled up in my cushy orange chair, sipping tea and loving Jesus. It's been quite some time since Sunday morning meant getting the whole family spruced up for a church service. . . . I am one of them, the non-goers. . . . The great news is that it is possible to be a Christian and not *go to church* but by *being the church* remain true to the call of Christ. . . . Is anyone up for a pickle-making party or a living-room song-writing session? Jesus will be there. . . . "If you want to start a church, just have a party in your house and see who shows up."[4]

Both Donald Miller and Kelly Bean are correct in one sense. Jesus is everywhere. He is there in our work, and he is there when we open our doors to throw a party. They are also correct in their view that every realm of life, not just church buildings on Sunday mornings, is sacred space. Every thought, word, and deed is meant to be an offering of worship to God. "Whether you eat or drink, or whatever you do," the Scriptures tell us, "do all to the glory of God."[5]

But would Jesus be in favor of a churchless Christianity?

The local church was God's idea. The Bible knows nothing of Christians who relate to God as isolated individuals or who see the local church as optional to their faith experience. As St. Cyprian once said, one cannot have God as his Father who does not have the church as his mother. Christians are members of Christ, but in being members of Christ they are also members of Christ's body, children in his family, and the sheep of his flock. Members, children, and sheep run together, not separately. The healthiest ones also have leaders who care for, nurture, protect, defend, teach, equip, and lead them. In the church, God has appointed deacons, elders, and pastors to be primary among those leaders.[6]

Since the local church was God's idea, is removing oneself from local church life for an alternative, custom-made, self-directed faith experience a legitimate consideration? As you may have guessed, my belief is that this is not a legitimate consideration for anyone who identifies as a follower of Jesus.

The New Testament Church

You might argue that, while the local church was God's idea, today's church bears little resemblance to God's original design. It can be tempting to leave the organized, local church in pursuit of something that better resembles the New Testament church. But do we really want something "more like the New Testament church"? In several incidences the New Testament church was actually less attractive, less authentic, less flexible, less loving, and less Christlike than the church of today. If anyone has ever been tempted to hit the eject button on the local church in favor of "piecing together a more robust faith experience," it was

Do we really want something "more like the New Testament church"?

people who were part of the New Testament church. Why else would the writer of Hebrews urge first-century Christians not to give up meeting together, "as is the habit of some"?[7] Even when the local church has become less than it should be, the biblical vision is to reform the church, not to abandon it.

How were things going in the local church in Corinth?

One of the most celebrated passages in the Bible is 1 Corinthians 13, famously known as the "love chapter." In this magnificent chapter, we are told that love is patient and kind. It does not envy or boast, and it is not arrogant or rude. It is not demanding or irritable, and it does not hold a grudge. It resists things that are wrong and celebrates things that are true. It bears, believes, hopes, and endures all things.

Wonderful, right?

But what if I told you that when Paul wrote to the Corinthians about love, he didn't have wedding ceremonies or cross-stitch art in mind? What if I told you that when Paul wrote to the Corinthians about love, he was actually rebuking them because they were lacking each of these attributes of love.

The Corinthian church, a prominent "New Testament church," was filled with problems. A brief journey through Paul's first letter to this community tells us that they were known for judging each other harshly, creating major divisions over minor theological issues, committing adultery, initiating frivolous law-suits, divorcing without biblical grounds, parading "Christian liberty" in front of people with bruised consciences, ignoring the needs of the poor—and the list goes on. The apostle Paul could have very easily written off this community. He could have very easily thrown in the towel.

Why *didn't* Paul throw in the towel on the New Testament church? For the same reason that Jesus didn't.

Church is family.

Membership in a local church means joining your imperfect self to many other imperfect selves to form an imperfect community that, through Jesus, embarks on a journey toward a better future . . . together.

Surprisingly, Paul begins his confrontational first letter to the Corinthians with affirmation and assurance. In spite of their manifold flaws, sins, inconsistencies, hypocrisies, and weaknesses, he is hopeful for them, not because they are stellar people but because Jesus is a stellar Savior. Jesus will complete the work that he began in them, and Paul knows this. So, instead of giving up on them, he doubles down on his involvement with them. Instead of shunning and shaming them, he speaks to them as his beloved brothers, sisters, sons, and daughters in the faith. He names them not according to their failures but according to their redemptive status, using words like "saints" and "sanctified." He thanks God always for them and reminds them that Jesus will sustain them until the end. Though they are messed up now, Jesus has a plan to transform them into people who are glorious and guiltless.

Paul looks at the broken local church and envisions beauty. He looks at the sinful local church and envisions sainthood. He looks at the undesirable local church and is overcome with desire for her flourishing. Paul thinks about the church in the same way that Jesus does. He thinks about the church as family. Daughters and sons of God, with whom he is well pleased. The bride of Christ, to whom he has betrothed himself forever. Sisters and brothers to one another, fellow heirs of the Kingdom.

Family.

As St. Augustine is said to have stated, the church may at times be a whore, but she is still my mother.

Becoming Christlike

Part of the Christian experience is learning to love difficult people just as Jesus loves us when we are difficult. This includes actively moving toward people we don't naturally like or enjoy. For churchless Christians, this central emphasis of Christian discipleship is rare. Why? Because, as Rick Warren says,

> The local church is the classroom for learning how to get along in God's family. It is a lab for practicing unselfish, sympathetic love. As a participating member you learn to care about others and share the experiences of others. . . . Only in regular contact with ordinary, imperfect believers can we learn real fellowship and experience the New Testament truth of being connected and dependent on each other.[8]

The hard and necessary work of reconciliation, peace-making, relational perseverance, and loving the unlovely is not something we generally gravitate to on our own or when we are creating a personal, custom-made spiritual experience. We need the inconvenient and costly demands of congregational living to shape that kind of love.

In *The Screwtape Letters*, C. S. Lewis says that if the devil wants to distract, discourage, and alienate a new Christian from his newfound faith in Jesus, the best way to do so is by tempting the new Christian to grow cynical toward his local church. In a letter to the young devil Wormwood, the experienced devil Screwtape says that the local church is one of the devil's most effective allies against "the Enemy" (God). All Wormwood has to do is get the new Christian to fixate on other people in the pews—especially those who have squeaky boots and double chins, and who sing off-key. The more unattractive and unimpressive the members of the local church appear to the Christian, the more cynical he will become toward the local church itself. And the more cynical he becomes toward the local church, the more cynical he will become about Christianity as a whole.

Anne Rice, author of the famous Vampire Chronicles, became a Christian later in life. Ten years into her life as a believer, Rice decided that she could no longer continue being part of the local church. In July of 2010, she wrote the following words to announce that she was quitting Christianity:

> Today I quit being a Christian. I'm out. I remain committed to Christ as always but not to being "Christian" or being part of Christianity. It's simply impossible for me to "belong" to this quarrelsome, hostile, disputatious, and deservedly infamous group. For ten years, I've tried. I've failed. I'm an outsider. My conscience will allow nothing else. . . . In the name of Christ, I quit Christianity. . . . My faith in Christ is central to my life. My conversion from a pessimistic atheist lost in a world I didn't understand, to an optimistic believer in a universe created and sustained by a loving God is crucial to me. But following Christ does not mean following His followers. Christ is infinitely more important than Christianity.[9]

In some ways, Rice's words sound noble and make a lot of sense. Who can argue with wanting to disassociate from a quarrelsome, hostile, disputatious, and deservedly infamous group? Having been a Christian for more than twenty-five years myself, I can tell you that being a Christian—especially the part that includes living in community with other Christians—can sometimes feel like being in a family with a thousand drunk uncles, to borrow the words of Justin McRoberts.[10]

Being a Christian can sometimes feel like being in a family with a thousand drunk uncles.

But is retreat really an option? Can we be in relationship with God while opting out of relationship with people—even difficult people—whom he loves? Can we claim Jesus as our elder brother while rejecting the church, whom he affectionately calls his bride?[11] Can we accept and receive his free offer of grace and patience and kindness and forgiveness and long-suffering toward us, while refusing to offer others the same?

What if Jesus had taken a similar position toward us?

"God shows his love for us in that *while we were still sinners, Christ died for us.*"[12]

We Don't Get to Choose Our Family Members

Groucho Marx famously said that he would never want to be part of any club that would have him as a member. What if we started there? What if we started with the recognition that nobody, including us, deserves a seat at the King's table, and that any welcome we have been given by God is all of grace? Would this change our posture toward the drunk uncles in our midst?

Like it or not, uncles are family.

We don't get to choose our family. Our family is chosen for us, and we make the very best of it because family members share a common heritage and a common inheritance.

Imagine a man meets the woman of his dreams. He soon discovers, to his delight, that he is also the man of her dreams. They spend time together, they fall in love, and he proposes marriage. She happily accepts. A month later, she invites him to attend her annual family reunion because she wants to introduce him to all her brothers, sisters, aunts, uncles, and cousins. At the family reunion, he discovers the unimaginable. Her father, previously unknown to him, wears boots that squeak. Her younger brother sings off-key. And her first cousin has a double chin. Furthermore, he discovers that several of her other relatives have high-pitched voices, voted for the wrong candidate, appreciate bad music, speak with unsophisticated accents, have bad breath, cheat on their tax returns, belch at the dinner table, are rude to the waiter, and aren't very interested in him as a person.

His fiancée is lovely. She is everything he has ever dreamed of and more. But the thought of a future with her family members is simply unbearable to him—because they are a quarrelsome, hostile, disputatious, and deservedly infamous group. He does not want to have anything to do with them.

"You know that I adore you," he says to her. "But if we are going to move forward with this wedding, you need to know that I don't ever want to see your mother, your father, your sisters, your brothers, your cousins, or any of your family members again. Can you marry me under these conditions?"

Of course she can't.

As troubling as it may be to the individualist in each of us, God and the church come to us as a package deal. God never calls us to himself in isolation. He calls us individually, but never as mere individuals. When he calls us to himself, he calls us into community. We don't get to choose, ultimately, who is part of that community any more than we get to choose the members of our own family.

> The church may at times be a whore, but she is still my mother.

Family members change over time. Family members go through seasons of being low-maintenance and also high-maintenance people. But because they are family, we stick with them through the good, the bad, and the ugly. They are family when they are at their best, and they are family when they are at their worst. They are family when relationships are easy, and they are family when relationships are difficult. They are family when we have offended them, and they are family when they have offended us. Either way, the nature of family is to stick together through thick and thin, for better or worse, for richer or poorer, in sickness and health.

This is how the church is meant to be as well.

Family is the chief metaphor that the Bible uses when it talks about the church. God is our Father. Jesus is our Husband. The Spirit is the Counselor to a redeemed, beloved, and often dysfunctional spiritual family. We are spiritual brothers and sisters and mothers and fathers and daughters and sons to one another. We didn't choose one another, but we have been given to one another by our Father in heaven, who intends for us to stay together and not hit the eject button when things get difficult or irritating or boring. And when we stay together, we are the better for it.

What Feels Difficult or Dull May Actually Be Glorious to God

By design, God created the church to be as diverse as possible. Our local church in Nashville, Christ Presbyterian, celebrates God's vision for a diverse spiritual family with the following words that describe our community:

> At Christ Presbyterian Church, we are a family that finds meaning in the truth, beauty, community, and mission of God. We are builders and baby boomers, gen-Xers and millennials, conservatives and progressives, educators and athletes, struggling doubters and committed believers, engineers and

artists, introverts and extroverts, healers and addicts, CEOs and homemakers, affluent and bankrupt, single and married, happy and hurting, lonely and connected, stressed out and carefree, private and public schoolers, PhDs and people with special needs, experts and students, saints and sinners.

These words attempt to capture one of the loveliest features of our church family: we celebrate and learn from our differences instead of dividing over them. We believe that the best expressions of community will happen when people come together with varying perspectives, personalities, cultures, and experiences.

This is Jesus' approach to community as well. If it were not, there would be no American church. Jesus was a first-century, Middle Eastern Jew who, according to the Bible, was not physically attractive, had no money, was sometimes homeless, hung around with sketchy people, and never spoke a word of English. Those of us who grew up in the West are different from Jesus in almost every way—generationally, geographically, ethnically, socioeconomically, vocationally, linguistically, and more. In a very real sense, we *are* "the ends of the earth" that he was talking about when he delivered the great commission to his disciples. In spite of how radically different and "other" we are to him, he has extended his welcome to us. He has invited us into his circle.

If this does not compel us to think twice about gravitating only toward people who think, look, dress, and live like us, what will?

Theologian Donald Carson writes:

Ideally . . . the church itself is not made up of natural "friends." It is made up of natural enemies. What binds us together is not common education, common race, common income levels, common politics, common nationality, common accents, common jobs, or anything else of that sort. Christians come together . . . because . . . they have all been loved by Jesus himself. . . . They are a band of natural enemies who love one another for Jesus' sake.[13]

Why would Dr. Carson say that it is *ideal* to be in a community that includes not only our natural friends but also our "natural enemies"—that is, those we don't naturally gravitate toward, those we don't naturally identify with, even those we don't naturally enjoy?

Sometimes it takes having differences, not understanding one another, and even being a little bit irritated by and bored with one another, to remind us that the church is a family and not a club. At its best, this family dynamic of the local church functions as God's fertile soil for growing us beyond mere tolerance toward true expressions of love and unity.

From Mere Tolerance to Love and Unity

Tolerance toward others in the local church is a good starting point, but it is not our final goal. To tolerate somebody is to merely put up with them, to live and let live. But it does not require us to be in relationship with the person. It carefully avoids all of the costs, inconveniences, and risks of love. Tolerance allows us to keep a safe, comfortable distance. Friendship, on the other hand, welcomes that somebody into our circle. Friendship takes us beyond tolerance to a common life together.

This is part of why I appreciate the ministry of the great pastor and preacher Dr. David Martyn Lloyd-Jones.

As a resident of Britain in the early twentieth century, Dr. Lloyd-Jones was well educated and privileged. As a leading physician, he lived in an affluent and class-conscious world. But when he sensed a call to pastoral ministry, Lloyd-Jones left medicine and high society to pastor a small church in a poor area by the shores of Wales. Reflecting on his time there, he would tell people about the joyful experience of talking about the Lord with the humblest fisherwoman. In many ways, the kinship he felt with his blue-collar parishioners gave him even greater joy than deep discussions about science, history, and philosophy with the privileged people he had grown up with.

Lloyd-Jones's experience reflects something beautiful. He was deeply conscious of the welcome that Jesus had extended to him. Because of this, it became natural for him to set aside man-made class distinctions and welcome all sorts of people into his life. Instead of being relationally narrow, he became relationally flexible. Instead of having only one kind of friend, he had many kinds of friends. Instead of welcoming only a select few into his inner circle, he welcomed all types of people. He did not merely tolerate the less affluent, less educated parishioners in Wales. He moved toward them, cherished them, and embraced them as his equals. He saw them as family.

Lloyd-Jones's experience shows us that there can be surprisingly wonderful friendships awaiting us with people we aren't naturally drawn to and who aren't naturally drawn to us. Friendship between opposites enables us to see that bonds formed around a shared love for Jesus are even greater than bonds formed around a shared interest, hobby, favorite sports team, income bracket, ethnicity, nationality, or bloodline. In the New Testament church, this special bond between Jews and Gentiles occurred across ethnic, ideological, and political boundaries. In Lloyd-Jones's experience, it occurred across educational, vocational, and economic boundaries. For others, it occurs across political and even geographical and language boundaries. The sheer diversity of the body of Christ is breathtaking in its ability to help us taste and savor the wonderful bond of a richly blended spiritual family. Having been united with Jesus, we have also been united to one another through him.

We Need the Church, and the Church Needs Us

Lloyd-Jones's experience with the church in Wales also teaches us how we are changed for the better by coming into contact with the "otherness" of one another. God has this magnificent way of working through our differences to bring out the best in each of us. This seems to be his primary strategy for taking the incomplete image of God in us and making it more complete. As we live in the company of people who are not like us, the unique expressions of God in them tend to rub off on us. As this happens, we become better, more whole, and more Christlike versions of ourselves. C. S. Lewis captures this idea beautifully in *The Four Loves* as he reflects on his and Ronald's (J. R. R. Tolkien's) friend Charles, whose death turned the trio into a less complete twosome:

> In each of my friends there is something that only some other friend can fully bring out. By myself I am not large enough to call the whole man into activity; I want other lights than my own to show all his facets. Now that Charles is dead, I shall never again see Ronald's reaction to a specifically Caroline [Charles-like] joke. Far from having more of Ronald, having him "to myself" now that Charles is away, I have less of Ronald. . . . We possess each friend not less but more as the number of those with whom we share him increases.[14]

Because of your uniqueness, you, and only you, are able to bring certain things out of me. Because of my uniqueness,

I, and only I, am able to bring certain things out of you. This is what I hope every Christian will consider. As irritating and unnecessary as the hand might seem to the eye, the eye cannot say to the hand, "I don't need you." Neither can the head say to the feet, "I don't need you."[15] God has designed us to be one body with many differences. The moment any of these parts is removed from the body, the body is weakened. Similarly, the moment a missing part is added back to the body, the body is strengthened and made more alive.

Every time I think about the man who was on his own disconnected, self-directed spiritual journey, or Donald Miller worshiping God in his work but not with a church, or Kelly Bean sipping tea at home on a Sunday morning, or Anne Rice's decision to quit Christianity, I am left to wonder. I wonder about all the people who are missing out on the uniqueness of the self-directed Christian, Donald Miller, Kelly Bean, and Anne Rice because they are absent from the church. When revolutionaries go missing, their absence causes this pastor to miss their presence. It makes me wonder what can be done, if anything, to bring them back home to the beloved, redeemed, dysfunctional family.

The messiness of the local church—let's just call it "Corinth"— needs the missing revolutionaries. Corinth needs the prophetic revolutionaries who are troubled by the messiness of Corinth. The judgmental saints in Corinth need gracious revolutionaries to show them a more beautiful way. The divisive saints in Corinth need unifying revolutionaries to help them major in the majors and minor in the minors. The adulterers in Corinth need pure-hearted revolutionaries to call them to account. The victims of adultery and wrongful divorce in Corinth need compassionate revolutionaries to love and support them and assure them at every turn that they are not alone. The bullied saints in Corinth need justice-oriented revolutionaries to stand between them and the bullies. The poor saints in Corinth need openhanded, compassionate revolutionaries to lift them out of a desperate state. The drunk uncles in Corinth need love and redemptive pressure from sober-minded revolutionaries who have a soft spot for drunk uncles and a vision for their sobriety. And the painfully ordinary people in Corinth—the ones with the squeaky boots, double chins, and off-key singing voices—need kindhearted revolutionaries to remind them that they are fearfully and wonderfully made.

I suppose what I am suggesting is that it would be beautiful, if not truly revolutionary, if the revolutionaries would consider joining Jesus in his mission to love Corinth back to life, versus the alternative of writing Corinth off.

Corinth needs the revolutionaries.

Something tells me that the revolutionaries need Corinth too.

Chapter Four

MONEY GUILT OR MONEY GREED?

*I think everybody should get rich and famous and do everything
they ever dreamed of so they can see that it's not the answer.*

—JIM CARREY

A FEW YEARS AGO, I was having breakfast with some friends
who worked in the finance industry. We were all living in New
York City, and the Great Recession was painfully impacting the
lives of everyone at the table. I listened carefully as each friend
shared his struggle.

One man, a Wall Street banker, told us about a harsh e-mail
that he had received from a woman in his church. In her e-mail,
she accused him of all sorts of horrible things—lining his own
pockets at the expense of people "who actually have to work
for a living," callously ignoring the poor, cheating the system
to protect the interests of the infamous "1 percent," scheming,
coveting, lying, stealing, and so on. She concluded her e-mail
by asking him how he could call himself a Christian when he
was *obviously* so greedy.

I was very bothered by the woman's approach. On one hand,
I sympathized with her concern about how the greed of a small

few can damage entire societies. I also sympathized with her concern that an individualistic, self-centered approach to wealth damages relationships and community. God gives us money to steward and share in order to promote the common good, not to hoard and spend solely on ourselves. However, the woman's concerns in this instance were severely misguided. She drew very negative conclusions about my friend simply because he was a bank executive. Her logic perhaps went something like this: "There are people at banks who are selfish and greedy. This guy works at a bank. Therefore, this guy is selfish and greedy." But this man is the furthest thing from selfish and greedy. He adopts orphaned children and gives tens of thousands of dollars each year to his church, nonprofit groups, and people who are in need. He lives in a home that is modest precisely *because* he has chosen to give so much of his wealth away. Part of the reason he chose to be a bank executive was to work from the inside to help reform the banking industry. He is one of the most honest, humble, and generous people I know.

Another man at the table shared about how his boss, the owner of a hedge fund, liked to drink expensive wine. Once, at a staff dinner, his boss opened a bottle that was valued at $25,000. I had two immediate internal reactions to this story. The first was to say that I could never enjoy a glass of wine from a bottle that was that expensive, because with each sip I would think, *There goes a year of college tuition. . . . There goes a new car. . . . There goes one month's pay for a nonprofit worker. . . . There goes an entire year's provision for a person living in the Third World. . . .* My second reaction was to be appalled. How could anyone think that spending this kind of money on wine was okay? How could anyone behave in such an opulent fashion? How could someone with this kind of money not think instead about how $25,000 could be used for ministry or given to the poor?

Then it dawned on me: in the same conversation I had felt defensive for my wealthy friend while judging another wealthy man whom I had never met.

Then I remembered Judas.

One day Mary, a disciple of Jesus, decided that she was going to do something opulent, over the top, and, by most people's standards, incredibly irresponsible. Taking a bottle of perfume valued at a full year's wages, Mary opened it and dumped it out on Jesus' feet. Judas, the keeper of the money bag, was infuriated by this. "Why wasn't this perfume sold and the money given to the poor? It was worth a year's wages." Jesus replied, "Leave her alone. . . . You will always have the poor among you, but you will not always have me."[1]

Jesus is more passionate than anyone about giving to the poor and about the dangers of affluence. He said it is harder for a rich man to enter God's Kingdom than it is for a camel to pass through the eye of a needle. He taught to be on guard against covetousness and that we cannot serve both God and money. He told his disciples to store up treasures in heaven and not on earth.[2] But he also decided it was okay for a woman to dump out a year's pay on *his* feet rather than donate it to the Temple treasury or give it to the poor. Jesus recognized a beautiful motive behind the woman's decision to lavish him with a luxurious gift. It was a gift compelled by love, so he received it gladly and enjoyed it fully. One might say that the perfume was Jesus' equivalent of an entire case of $25,000 wine.

Wealth Is Not the Problem

With all the many warnings in the Bible about the potential snares of wealth, there are also many passages that speak positively about prosperity. The Garden of Eden was a Garden of Paradise. Abraham, father of the faithful and a friend of God, had great wealth. God led the Israelites into a land flowing with milk and honey. When Solomon asked God for wisdom, God made him wise and also lavished him with wealth. Job, the most righteous man in the land, was also the wealthiest man in the land. The writer of Ecclesiastes says that it is good to enjoy the wealth that God gives to us. King David prayed that the sons and daughters of Israel would be fit for a palace, with full granaries and sheep numbering in the thousands. The prophets urged the rich to lift the poor out of their poverty, because poverty is an expression of the world's brokenness. Jesus became poor so that through his poverty we might become rich, and he promises to share with us his eternal inheritance that will never spoil or fade away. Jesus says that his Father's house has many mansions, and he has gone to prepare a place there for his people. In the new heaven and new earth, Jesus' people will walk on streets of gold and live in a city adorned with every kind of jewel.[3]

So which is it? Is Jesus in favor of wealth or is he opposed to it? Furthermore, how should we be thinking about wealth?

The subject of wealth is not as cut and dried as we might think. There is room in God's economy for nuance on the subject; the Bible is full of affirmations of people who are both poor and rich, who accumulate wealth and who give wealth away, who enjoy God's provision and who provide for others through sacrificial giving.

The Secret of Contentment

When the Bible talks about prosperity, having or not having wealth is never the chief concern. The chief concern for the rich and for the poor is whether our hearts are content with what God has given to us. The Bible helps us understand that this kind of contentment—the kind that stays intact during prosperous times as well as during times of scarcity—is reachable only for those who see God himself as their true wealth. Contentment grows as we live from the truth that *God* is our ultimate portion, our ultimate share, and our ultimate inheritance.[4]

The Bible invites us to be *satisfied* even when we have only a little, because our deepest need—to have God be with us and for us—has been richly met. This is why Paul was able to say even from jail that he had learned the secret of being content in any and every situation.

But Paul doesn't just say he can be content with little. He also says he can be content with much:

> I have learned in whatever situation I am to be content.
> I know how to be brought low, and I know how to
> abound. In any and every circumstance, I have learned
> the secret *of facing plenty* and hunger, *abundance*
> and need. I can do all things through him who
> strengthens me.[5]

Paul implies that it's not just hunger and need that pose a challenge to contentment; so do plenty and abundance. Material wealth in a fallen world is surrounded by paradox. Wealth provides for our needs, yet it can become poison if we become obsessed with it. It promises to fulfill us, yet it can leave us empty. It promises to satisfy, yet it can leave us hungry for more. It is morally neutral, yet it can be harmful. It is a gift to enjoy, yet it should be given away freely.

> The chief concern for the rich and for the poor is whether our hearts are content with what God has given to us.

How can we ensure that our relationship with money is healthy? What does it look like for contentment to grow and for greed to diminish in our hearts? How can we enjoy the wealth God has entrusted to us—whether a little or a lot—while also living generous lives?

A Hidden Sickness

Outrage about greed is loud and clear in our culture. High unemployment rates, a growing economic gap between the haves and the have-nots, more college graduates moving back in with their parents, mounting national debts, skyrocketing inflation, and poverty are only a few reasons why people are angry.

We are also angry toward people—*other* people—who seem irresponsible and selfish with their wealth. The woman who sent the e-mail to my Wall Street friend was outraged. Why? Because he worked for a bank, and everyone knows that people who work for banks ruin economies. I was outraged about the hedge fund owner's $25,000 bottle of wine. Why? Because everyone knows that people who drink $25,000 bottles of wine don't care about us "average" people.

But are we really average?

Are we truly somewhere in the middle of the pack when it comes to wealth?

If we have more than one change of clothing, eat more than one meal per day, and have a roof over our heads, chances are that we are not somewhere in the middle of the pack. Chances are we are not average at all.

Did you know that more than half of the world's population lives on less than $2.50 per day? What would more than half of the world's population think about the size of my retirement account? Or the $20 bottle of wine I shared with friends last night? Or the $60 dinner I enjoyed with my wife over the weekend?

These questions put things in perspective for me.

I am not a fan of money guilt. I am not a fan of shame or

of making people feel bad for being wealthy. Rather, my goal here is to raise an important question. Why am I appalled at a $25,000 bottle of wine relative to my own income, but not appalled at my $20 bottle of wine relative to the income of more than half of the world's population? Should I be appalled at both? Should I be appalled at neither? Where should I draw the line?

> If we have more than one change of clothing, eat more than one meal per day, and have a roof over our heads, chances are that we are not somewhere in the middle of the pack.

Consider this testimony from Sam Polk, a former Wall Street trader, as he reflects in the *New York Times* on how blind he had become to his own money sickness:

> In my last year on Wall Street my bonus was $3.6 million—and I was angry because it wasn't big enough. I was 30 years old, had no children to raise, no debts to pay, no philanthropic goal in mind. I wanted more money for exactly the same reason an alcoholic needs another drink: I was addicted. . . . It's staggering to think that in the course of five years, I'd gone from being thrilled at my first bonus—$40,000— to being disappointed when, my second year at the hedge fund, I was paid "only" $1.5 million.[6]

Sam Polk's story puts a spotlight on a pervasive problem that few of us are prepared to admit. Our greed can usually be traced back to dissatisfaction about what we have in comparison to others. A five-figure wage earner is bothered by the relative affluence of the six-figure wage earners in his life. Similarly, the six-figure wage earner is bothered by the relative affluence of the seven-figure wage earners in her life. We tell ourselves that if we could only reach the next income bracket, we would be content. However, once we get to the next bracket, we start wishing ourselves into the next bracket after that. As a result, we carry a perpetual disappointment with where we are economically. C. S. Lewis believes that our problem is just as much competitive and envy based as it is economic. According to Lewis, it is not that we want to be rich, as much as it is that we want to be *richer* than the next person.[7]

If we are going to be part of the solution to the greed problem, we really need to look at ourselves first. Do I see my own tendency to compare myself with others, and in so doing never be satisfied? Do I see my own susceptibility to greed? In what ways has a pure enjoyment of God's material blessings morphed into a love of money, which is a root of all kinds of evil and grief? In what ways have I become zealous to remove specks from the eyes of others while missing the log in my own?[8]

Symptoms of Greed: Hoarding and Spending

Once we reach a certain age, medical experts recommend a yearly checkup to examine vital signs, blood chemistry, and other health indicators. The annual checkup is important because certain diseases can be detected only through careful, "under the hood" examination. It is possible to feel healthy and have a life-threatening disease at the same time.

Jesus tells us that money sickness, or greed, is a universal disease for which everybody is at risk. The "super rich" are not the only people who are susceptible. We all think that greed is a huge problem. But we rarely think that it is *our* problem. It is easy for us to see greed in others, but we have a hard time seeing it in ourselves. We are all susceptible to this hidden disease. Most of us have it, yet many of us don't detect it.

An older minister once told me that in his almost forty years of pastoral ministry, people had confessed all sorts of sins to him—sex addiction, adultery, theft, dishonesty, drunkenness, and unbelief—but not one person had ever confessed to having a problem with greed.

In 1999, Harvard economist Juliet Schor did a study of American spending habits. Schor's research revealed that two-thirds of Americans with an annual income exceeding $75,000 (over $107,000 in today's dollars after inflation) felt they wouldn't be satisfied until their salaries were 50 to 100 percent higher.[9]

Money can have a blinding effect.

When we are sick with greed, we usually cannot see the sickness in ourselves. How do we identify it? What are its symptoms? I believe that there are chiefly two: hoarding money *for* ourselves and spending money almost exclusively *on* ourselves.

Some of us are extremely tight-fisted with money, hoarding it in order to feel safe. My wife could tell you that one of my triggers, one of the things that can preoccupy my thoughts in an unhealthy way, is anxiety about what the future holds with respect to finances. Will there be enough for my kids' college educations, for old age, for unexpected sickness and tragedy? Sometimes I can get so anxious about these things that they overwhelm me. When the bank account seems low, I feel panic and fear—the irrational kind. When it seems more built up, I have confidence—the misplaced kind.

> Our greed can usually be traced back to dissatisfaction about what we have in comparison to others.

And yet I am a contradiction. I also spend money on things that I do not need. I have more pairs of jeans and shoes than I am able to wear. I have several Mac computers and i-Things when I could get along easily with just one of each. I have a top-of-the-line Martin guitar and a top-of-the-line Gibson—even though I am a mediocre guitarist at best and will never take a stage to do anything but preach. Last year I sold a mechanically sound, paid-for car in order to buy a new Jeep Wrangler.

Is it wrong to have these things? Is it wrong to enjoy them? Again, no it is not. We have seen that the Bible allows for and even encourages the enjoyment of wealth and material goods. It is not money that the Bible says is a root of evil, but the *love* of money. Nicodemus and Joseph of Arimathea were two prominent members of society and were also disciples of Jesus. As a tax collector, Matthew was likely a man of significant means, as was Luke, a physician. Lydia owned a home that was large enough to host a local church. King David played a harp (perhaps his equivalent to my Martin guitar) to calm the spirit of King Saul. Solomon lived in a luxurious palace and was arrayed with fine jewels and expensive clothing. Adam and Eve lived in Paradise, the garden of delight that God created and called "very good." God invites us to enjoy and benefit from his creation as well as the physical or material goods that money can buy. In that sense, we are "materialist" beings.

But it is dangerously easy for materialist beings to become materialistic.

How do we know we are at risk of being materialistic? We are at risk when we find ourselves hoarding money in order to feel safe. We are equally at risk when we find ourselves in a pattern of spending money almost exclusively on ourselves . . . especially when we spend it on things we do not need to impress the people around us.

It is healthy to ask myself why I have four of this thing and three of that thing and two of the other thing and this particular vehicle—which, if I'm being honest, just *might* be indicative of a midlife crisis. There are sometimes good reasons to own these sorts of luxuries—after all, God invites us to enjoy wealth as well as to share wealth with others. But we must examine our motives carefully. Are we legitimately saving wealth or do we have a hoarding sickness? Are we legitimately enjoying wealth or do we have a spending sickness?

In other words, have we moved from having wealth to placing our hope in wealth?

Wealth Is Not the Answer

I have never met anyone who wanted their epitaph to read, "He spent his weekends at the office, ignoring his loved ones, losing sleep, and earning huge bonuses." Yet I have met many men and women who live this way, as if money is the answer to all the world's problems and is worth sacrificing other things that are valuable. For example, the pursuit of money leads many people to neglect and even forfeit more important pursuits such as health and relationships. Space for both God and loved ones is crowded out by a preoccupation with the next deal or bonus. Even when these people are present physically, they are not present relationally. When they reach the end of their lives, what they thought would be a pot of gold at the end of the rainbow is actually fool's gold.

Woody Allen once said that money is better than poverty, if only for financial reasons. He said this to get a laugh, but in reality this is no laughing matter. If not handled with care, money will turn on us and grab us around the neck. It will let us down instead of lifting us up. It will fail to deliver on the promises it makes to us.

Some of the world's wealthiest people have experienced letdown when they hit their coveted "number." The story goes that having made billions in the oil industry, John D. Rockefeller was asked how much money was enough. His answer was, "One more dollar." Jim Carrey, a rich and famous actor, said that being rich and famous did not solve any of his problems. Quarterback Tom Brady, after winning three Super Bowl victories, marrying the world's top supermodel, and achieving an annual household income of $76 million per year, said in an interview that this couldn't be all that there is, that there has to be something more. Kobe Bryant, who by the age of twenty-four already had millions of dollars, a beautiful wife, and a beachfront mansion, told *Newsweek* that he did not believe in happiness. Madeline Levine, a psychiatrist who works closely with teens from affluent homes, says that many teens share the same struggle. In her book *The Price of Privilege*, she writes:

> America's newly identified at-risk group is preteens and
> teens from affluent, well-educated families. In spite
> of their economic and social advantages, ["children
> of affluence"] experience among the highest rates of
> depression, substance abuse, anxiety disorders, somatic
> complaints, and unhappiness of any group of children
> in this country.[10]

How can this be? How can wealth, thought of by many as the *answer* to the world's problems, become for many a *cause* of more problems than it solves? The problem does not lie in having or spending money as much as it does with how our hearts relate to it. Jesus says,

> Be on your guard against all covetousness, for one's life
> does not consist in the abundance of his possessions.[11]

> No servant can serve two masters, for either he will
> hate the one and love the other, or he will be devoted
> to the one and despise the other. You cannot serve
> God and money.[12]

Paul writes,

> If we have food and clothing, with these we will [and can] be content. But those who *desire* to be rich fall into temptation, into a snare, into many senseless and harmful desires that plunge people into ruin and destruction. For the love of money is a root of all kinds of evils.[13]

All these verses are getting at essentially one thing: Jesus, not money, is the answer to our quest for safety and validation. When our souls are empty, it becomes natural to have distorted notions and experiences of wealth. When a healthy relationship with money turns into a love for money, when wealth turns into greed, when enjoyment of material things turns into materialism, our souls become *more* impoverished and empty, not less. Because our souls are crafted in the image of a great and magnificent God, they can never be filled with such a small thing as money. Only Jesus can fill an empty soul.[14]

> When our souls are empty, it becomes natural to have distorted notions and experiences of wealth.

Whether we have a little or a lot, then, we must be on our guard against *all* covetousness—whether the hoarding or spending variety. This involves discerning where we are relying on money to do for us what only Jesus can. It involves inviting others to speak into our lives on these issues. And it involves examining our relationship with money against what Scripture says about how we are to earn it, save it, spend it, and give it.

Gaining More by Having Less

Let's also consider what happens to the human soul when it is filled with the currency of Jesus' truth, beauty, grace, forgiveness, and love. When our souls derive safety and validation from Jesus, we tend to take on the attributes of his generous, self-giving love. When this happens, we also experience joy.

I will never forget hearing Joni Eareckson Tada tell the story about one of her visits to a poor village in Ghana. Joni and a few of her American friends decided to attend a worship service at a small church in the village. One of the first things that Joni noticed was that the most joyful and boisterous moment in the service was when it was time for congregants to contribute to the offering. The congregants, many of them among the poorest people in the world, found meaning and happiness in releasing whatever small amount they had to offer into the collection basket. They deeply believed Jesus' promise that it is more blessed, or "happy," to give than it is to receive.[15]

Joni also noticed that it was not in spite of, but because of, their lack of wealth that these worshipers from Ghana had so much joy. At one point in the service, a woman stood up to welcome those who were present. As she spoke, she was moved to share these words with Joni and her friends: "Welcome, our American friends, to Ghana, where we have joy because we need Jesus more."

We have joy . . . because we need Jesus more.

Is this kind of joy possible for those who are not materially poor? Can we be transformed into joyful and generous givers who are satisfied with having less? Before we start liquidating our bank accounts, there is something else for us to consider. Before Jesus invites us to participate in his generosity, he first invites us to receive and enjoy his generosity toward us. This was the path to joy for the worshipers in Ghana. It is also the path to joy for us.

Rich toward God

In his parable of the rich fool, Jesus says that greedy hearts are healed when they become generous or "rich" toward God. He identifies the root causes of greed, which are anxiety and fear. He tells his disciples not to be anxious about food or clothing or anything else, because life is more than these things. He reminds them that God takes care of the birds and causes the lilies in the field to grow. If God takes care of the birds and the lilies, how much more will God take care of us? Then he tells them not to let their hearts be troubled and not to fear, because their Father in heaven knows what they need before they ask him. If they seek God's Kingdom and righteousness first, God will make sure that all of their needs—as he defines "needs"—are met.

Jesus assures and comforts his money-sick disciples instead of shaming them. Then, he lovingly tells them not to be afraid:

> Fear not, little flock, for it is your Father's good
> pleasure to give you the kingdom. Sell your possessions,
> and give to the needy. Provide yourselves with
> moneybags that do not grow old, with a treasure in the
> heavens that does not fail, where no thief approaches
> and no moth destroys. For where your treasure is, there
> will your heart be also.[16]

Jesus invites us to be generous because God is generous, and because our money was never *our* money in the first place. God is the owner of wealth, and we are the managers. He invites us to use and unleash and share his wealth according to what matters most to him. These priorities include, but are not limited to, providing for the needs of those who depend on us, saving for the future, and giving generously to God's Kingdom causes, especially to the church and the poor. When we arrange our financial lives around these and similar priorities, we actively "seek God's Kingdom." As we do this, God meets our heartfelt need of being able to participate in something enduring and meaningful.

But when it comes to giving, what is the right amount? How

much are the followers of Jesus supposed to give? How much is too little and how much is too much? These questions are important, but there is no one-size-fits-all answer. Our level of giving depends on our situation.

For example, Nicodemus and Joseph of Arimathea, two very wealthy men, anointed Jesus' dead body with seventy-five pounds of spices. The cash value of these spices was nearly one hundred years' wages for the average worker. Wealthy Zacchaeus gave 50 percent of his earnings away. Similarly, there are many who have been blessed with the ability to far exceed the biblical starting point of the 10 percent tithe.[17] Some, like C. S. Lewis and Rick Warren, have been able to give away the vast majority (even up to 90 percent) of their earnings to their churches, to the poor, and to other Kingdom causes.

But C. S. Lewis and Rick Warren are in the minority. Their situations are not common. What about those of us who earn less? Scripture guides us as well. The middle-income Pharisees gave 10 percent to the Temple and then gave freewill offerings, as they were able, to the poor and to other Kingdom concerns. The poor widow gave just a single mite, not much more than a penny in value—a gesture that moved Jesus to call her offering "the greatest gift" because the mite represented her entire net worth. The poor widow wanted all of her treasure to be with God because God had captured all of her heart.

A Generosity Crisis

According to a recent study reported in *Relevant* magazine, only 10 to 25 percent of the typical American congregation tithes (that is, gives the biblical starting point of 10 percent) to the church, the poor, and Kingdom causes. The same report concluded that if the remaining 75 to 90 percent of American Christians began to tithe regularly, then global hunger, starvation, and death from preventable diseases could be relieved within five years. Additionally, illiteracy could be eliminated, the world's water and sanitation issues could be solved, all overseas mission work could be fully funded, and over $100 billion per year would be left over for additional ministry.[18]

But because 75 to 90 percent of American Christians are reluctant to give wealth away in biblical proportions, the generosity crisis remains. Put starkly, this means that 75 to 90 percent of American Christians—those who collectively represent the wealthiest Christians in the world—are money-sick.

Should this drive us to guilt and shame? Of course not. Jesus took care of our shame on the cross. But the epidemic of hoarding money when God says to give it away, and spending money disproportionately on ourselves when God says we should also be sharing it liberally, should drive us toward something, or *someone*. It should make us hungry for a money-sickness cure.

God has given us a way to start: the tithe. Just as the Sabbath command reminds us that God grants seven days of provision as we put in six days of work and one day of rest, the tithe reminds us that God is going to meet 100 percent of our needs as we return 10 percent of our regular income back to him.

> If American Christians began to tithe regularly, global hunger, starvation, and death from preventable diseases could be relieved within five years.

The tithe reminds us that God is our provider, that he is sufficient to meet our needs, and that he, not money, is the ultimate answer to our soul-thirst for safety and validation.

Did you know that tithing is the single act in which God invites us to *test* him?

> Will man rob God? Yet you are robbing me. But you say, "How have we robbed you?" In your tithes and

contributions. You are cursed with a curse, for you are robbing me, the whole nation of you. Bring the full tithe into the storehouse. . . . And thereby put me to the test, says the LORD of hosts, if I will not open the windows of heaven for you and pour down for you a blessing until there is no more need. . . . Then all nations will call you blessed, for you will be a land of delight, says the LORD of hosts.[19]

These are sharp words, but with promises attached. God's sharpness is compelled by an eagerness to demonstrate that he, not money, is our answer to feeling safe and cared for.

The clear message of Scripture is that when our net worth gets below our comfort level, whether through tithing or through circumstances that God decides are best for us, we, too, are given an opportunity, counterintuitive though it may be, to find joy in needing Jesus more. A shrinking net worth can be one of God's greatest hidden blessings. True freedom is found in the realization that "everything minus Jesus equals nothing" and "Jesus plus nothing equals everything." But sometimes, especially for those of us who have been given much, it takes having less material wealth to realize that the true wealth is found in Jesus.

Trusting God to care for us frees us to give to others and enjoy what he has given. Trusting God for our present and future security frees us to move toward him and others with open hearts and open hands.

How do we know that true riches are found in Jesus? The answer to this question is found in how committed Jesus is to take care of us. On the cross he gave up all of his wealth—not just 10 percent but 100 percent of it—so he could have us. He became poor so that we, through his poverty, might become rich. Jesus was liquidated of his assets—literally!—as he bled out for us on the cross. Because of his generosity, we have been validated, and we have been made safe in the deepest, truest sense.

When we begin to see this, our hearts become full. As our hearts become full, mirroring God's generous heart will be a natural outcome.

And we will have joy . . . because we will need him more.

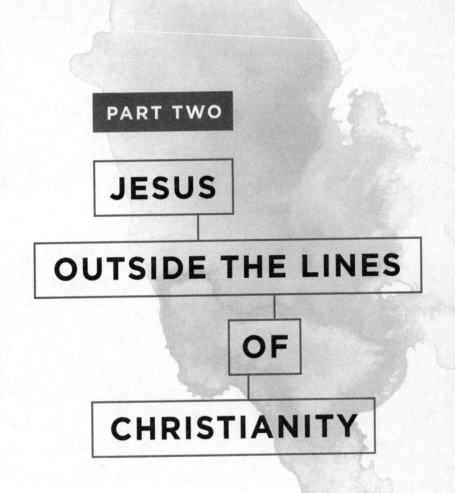

PART TWO

JESUS

OUTSIDE THE LINES

OF

CHRISTIANITY

Chapter Five

AFFIRMATION OR CRITIQUE?

The relativism which is not willing to speak about truth but only about "what is true for me" is an evasion of the serious business of living. It is the mark of a tragic loss of nerve in our contemporary culture. It is a preliminary symptom of death.

—LESSLIE NEWBIGIN

RECENTLY I WAS DOING RESEARCH FOR A SERMON on Jesus' conversation with Nicodemus about being "born again." I came across a couple of alarming quotes that struck me as also funny. The first was from a San Francisco journalist named Herb Caen, who says that "the trouble with born-again Christians is that they are an even bigger pain the second time around." The second was from Katharine Whitehorn, a British journalist, who wonders, "Why do born-again people so often make you wish they'd never been born the first time?"[1]

Usually when people say these kinds of things about my people—and by "my people" I mean Christians—I laugh, if for no other reason than that it's good not to take oneself or one's tribe too seriously. It is healthy to laugh at ourselves and, if the shoe actually fits, give a conceding nod to our critics. Still, negative caricatures about "my people" can also be sobering because sometimes the shoe fits a little bit too well.

While I don't know exactly why these journalists spoke like this about Christians, I suspect that at least part of it relates to an observation Philip Yancey once made in an interview about his book *What's So Amazing about Grace?*

> When I ask people, "What is a Christian?" they don't usually respond with words like love, compassion, grace; usually they describe a person who's *anti-*something. Jesus was not primarily known for what he was against. He was known for serving people who had needs, feeding people who were hungry, and giving water to the thirsty. If we [Christians] were known primarily for that, then we could cut through so many divisions. . . . *Christians* often have a bad reputation. People think of Christians as uptight and judgmental. Odd, I thought, that [our version of Christianity] has come to convey the opposite of God's intent, as it's lived out through us.[2]

I think we Christians should listen humbly, thoughtfully, and carefully to people who express their misgivings about us. Somehow in our efforts to "speak the truth" we have too often forgotten about the love that God intends to undergird the truth. We have forgotten to let our speech "always be gracious, seasoned with salt, so that [we] may know how [we] ought to answer each person."[3]

Jesus was offensive to smug, judgmental, religious people. He was a breath of fresh air to broken, nonreligious people. Can the same things be said about his followers today? If not, what are the reasons why? Why are there still people who think that "Christian" and "anti-something" are one and the same? More important, is there a path forward that could reverse this common impression?

I believe there are things that can help "my people" move past any negative caricatures, bad attitudes, or combative postures that have sidelined us from the path of Jesus. I am hopeful that we live in a time in which God is doing a new work in us—one that stirs us toward a more affirming manifesto, something that resembles the Prayer of St. Francis in both word and deed:

> Lord, make us instruments of your peace. Where
> there is hatred, let us sow love; where there is injury,
> pardon; where there is discord, union; where there is
> doubt, faith; where there is despair, hope; where there
> is darkness, light; where there is sadness, joy. Grant
> that we may not so much seek to be consoled as to
> console; to be understood as to understand; to be loved
> as to love. For it is in giving that we receive; it is in
> pardoning that we are pardoned; and it is in dying that
> we are born to eternal life. Amen.

And yet a Christian may ask, "Doesn't critique play some sort of role in the life of a believer?" Shouldn't Christians speak truth to power, bring a prophetic word to those who have turned from God, warn people about sin and judgment, and the like? Shouldn't Christians shine as light in dark places, call people to repent and believe, and go into the world and teach people to obey everything that Jesus commanded? Shouldn't we expect that as we do these things there will be people who treat us like enemies and who say, "I do not like your Christians?"

Yes, we should. Even when done in love, speaking the truth, shining as light in darkness, and taking up a cross to follow Jesus will draw certain forms of opposition. But if people are going to get upset with us, let's at least make sure they are the same types of people who got upset with Jesus.

The lepers and the crooks and the drunks and the gluttons and the sexually promiscuous people and the sinners and the nonchurchgoers, to be clear, did *not* oppose or get upset with Jesus. These people were drawn to him, and in being drawn to him they were drawn to his community. There was something about him that these people knew they needed. There was something about him that made these people feel that as long as Jesus was nearby, hope was possible and everything might actually turn out okay.

Those who opposed Jesus the most were the committed "church people"—the priests, the Levites, the Bible scholars, the people who fasted and prayed and gave their tithes faithfully at the Temple and made sure everybody knew about it. But Jesus was not impressed. He gave them no applause for their piety and their dutiful good works. Rather, he critiqued them sharply and often; told them they were not children of Abraham but children of the devil; called them blind guides who don't practice what they preach, narcissists who honor themselves instead of God, whitewashed tombs and hypocrites who neglect justice and mercy, who shed innocent blood, and whose religion is smoke and mirrors and whose devotion is a self-indulgent show. To make matters worse, Jesus brought irreligious outcasts—the tax collectors and sinners and gluttons and drunks—into his inner ring. He welcomed them and ate with them. He called them his friends. He knew their names and their stories. Instead of casting them out, he drew them in. And he made sure that the committed church people heard loudly and clearly that the crooks and prostitutes were entering God's Kingdom ahead of them—particularly the crooks and

If people are going to get upset with us, let's at least make sure they are the same types of people who got upset with Jesus.

prostitutes who had a sense of their own moral and spiritual bankruptcy.[4]

So there you have it. Jesus affirmed some and he critiqued others. And he did so in ways that most would least expect. Is this also true of us?

To Be Human Is to Need Encouragement

In his book *How Children Raise Parents*, counselor and author Dan Allender says that to nurture a life-giving home environment, parents must be aware of two questions that their children are always subconsciously asking. All children ask both questions daily as they consider the freedoms and boundaries given to them by their parents. The first question is *Do my parents love me?* The second is *Will my parents let me have whatever I want?* Well-parented children know that the answer to the first question is always yes and the answer to the second question is always no.[5]

As the father of two girls, I can attest to the truth of Allender's assessment. As soon as they leave the womb, children are going to test the limits of what they can and cannot do and of what they can and cannot have. And, most especially, children want to know that their parents love them.

From early on, Patti and I longed to create a secure home for our daughters in which they always knew they were loved. As Tim Keller likes to say, we determined to "catch them doing good" anytime we had an opportunity. We wanted our daughters to grow up feeling affirmed, valued, and cherished as unique and amazing carriers of the image of God. But we discovered early on that not even this level of praise and affirmation was enough to fully convince our daughters of our unconditional love and acceptance. For example, one of our daughters would always ask a specific question after being disciplined: "Daddy [or Mommy], are you happy at me?"

We praised her every day and night. We caught her doing good every chance we could. Yet all it took was one act of disobedience, one brief moment of discipline, one little critique for the unsettling insecurity to creep in that perhaps she was somehow not so beautiful or special or loved anymore. *Daddy, are you happy at me?*

I remember watching an interview with Mariah Carey, who at the time was in her late twenties and had accumulated more number-one hits than anyone in music except for Elvis Presley and the Beatles. The interviewer asked Carey if there was anything left for her to accomplish. She sat quietly for a moment, then replied, "Happiness." The interviewer was thrown off by the answer and asked how this could be true. How, with such great success and so much talent and so many hits and so many fans and so much applause and so much money, can you not be happy? Carey did not have to think about how to answer the second question. Right away, she looked at the interviewer and said she could hear a thousand praises and then just one criticism, and the one criticism would overrule the thousand praises and wreck her emotionally.

What is it about the human heart that makes us so sensitive to criticism? Why are we so undone by it? Why does it unravel us as it does? Why does a little girl lose her emotional equilibrium in a moment of parental discipline, or a megastar musician forget who she is because of one criticism? Or why, when a text message or the subject line of an e-mail says, "We need to talk" (or for us pastors, "About your sermon") are we struck with a sudden feeling of doom? Why do we spend hours in the gym or in front of the mirror or online meticulously editing our social media profiles? Why is the perfect "selfie" such a large part of how we present ourselves to the world? Why do we live in constant disequilibrium about what our real or imagined critics might say about us?

Consider this excerpt from a book by Donald Miller:

Last year I caught an interview with Tom Arnold regarding his book *How I Lost Five Pounds in Six Years*. The interviewer asked why he had written the book, and I was somewhat amazed at the honesty of Arnold's answer. The comedian stated that most entertainers are in show business because they are broken people, looking for affirmation. "The reason I wrote this book," Tom Arnold said, "is because I wanted something out there so people would tell me they liked me. It's the reason behind almost everything I do." I have to tell you, after that, I really liked Tom Arnold.[6]

After that, I really liked Tom Arnold too. Most would agree that this kind of honesty about the human condition is courageous and disarming, but it is much more. It is relieving and life giving, especially to people who are prepared to admit that they don't have it all together. Why don't we just admit it? We are frail and afraid. We are unimpressed with ourselves because we are not what we think we are supposed to be. So many of our goals and dreams and efforts end in anticlimax. And yet, we still crave affirmation.

Some call this neediness. Others call it the image of God. We have been created to mirror him, which means that a receptivity to and a desire for praise is deeply ingrained in us.

If God is magnificent (he is), if our chief end is to glorify and enjoy him *in* his magnificence (it is), and if the natural world also exists for this same purpose (it does),[7] then what does that say about human beings who are made in God's image, of whom God is always mindful, and whom God has made "a little lower than the heavenly beings and crowned him with glory and honor . . . [and] given him dominion over the works of

[God's] hands . . . [and] put all things under his feet?"[8] If God is pleased with praise and affirmation from his people—never needy of it, but always pleased with it—should we who bear his image not also be pleased with and desirous of praise and affirmation ourselves?

This longing for affirmation makes sense. Both existentially real and biblically true, it is the reason we Christians should be the most affirming people in the world. Rather than rushing to find fault, we should proactively seek opportunities to catch others doing good and to encourage (literally, "put courage into") others by verbalizing the ways that we are "happy at them"—whether they believe as we do or not. Jesus certainly understood this, and so must we.

Affirmation without Caveats

Jesus had an extremely high view of the law of God—so high that in his Sermon on the Mount he interpreted the Ten Commandments in an even stricter way than the scribes and Pharisees did. In every way, we fall woefully short of the bar he set in his life and teaching. Even our most righteous deeds, when measured against Jesus' standard of holiness, are like dirty rags.[9] Yet, even in the midst of brokenness and failure we find Jesus extending life-giving affirmation.

Jesus Affirmed His Followers

Peter, for example, had a few bouts with racism and cowardice, not to mention zero impulse control in certain social situations. Yet it was Peter to whom Jesus gave the name "The Rock" because Peter's confession that Jesus is the Christ would become the bedrock upon which the entire church would be built.[10] Later, when Jesus needed a ministry of presence and prayer from his friends, Peter fell asleep. When he needed Peter to walk alongside him in his darkest hour, Peter abandoned and denied him—not just once, but three times. Yet when the women showed up at the tomb, the risen Jesus made certain that the most affirming word of all was sent to the one who had committed this shameful betrayal: "Go, tell his disciples *and Peter* that [Jesus] is going before you to Galilee. There you will see him, just as he told you."[11]

And Peter. You just have to love Jesus.

Though his disciples made all sorts of mistakes, and though Jesus did not turn a blind eye to these mistakes, he saw the disciples fundamentally as his friends, his companions, his partners, and his trusted ambassadors. He wanted them to know that he approved of them, that he had high hopes for them, and that God would complete the work God had begun in them. He wanted them to know that he *liked* them. He wanted them to know that he was happy at them.

Jesus Affirmed His Non-followers, Too

I love to say positive things about people who don't share my Christian faith. In my sermons, teaching, and writing, it is not uncommon for me to quote an existentialist philosopher like Camus or Nietzsche, celebrate the work of a painter like Mark Rothko or Jackson Pollock, refer to books by business leaders such as Jim Collins or Steve Jobs, draw from the imaginations of storytellers like Arthur Miller or Virginia Woolf, delight in the music of Ray LaMontagne or Kanye West or the Indigo Girls, or engage with films, TV shows, and other art forms that include secular themes. Why would a minister assume such an affirming posture toward secular people and secular ideas?

There are two reasons. The first is that I believe non-Christians say and do a lot of praiseworthy things. Non-Christians as well as Christians create beauty, speak words that are true, and perform deeds that serve the common good. This should be celebrated.

The second reason I like to affirm non-Christians is that Jesus went around affirming non-Christians all the time. He did the same with several men and women who identified themselves as believers, or who were moving toward belief, but who also lived inconsistently with his teaching and his ethics. Jesus, the author of all truth, beauty, and goodness, was quick to affirm expressions of truth, beauty, and goodness wherever he saw them. He shone a spotlight on the image of God in people anywhere the image of God would come out of hiding. Oftentimes such affirmation was his "step one" in the process of redeeming someone.

John 4 tells about Jesus' encounter with a Samaritan woman at Jacob's well. This woman was promiscuous, and Jesus pointed out that she had been with five men and that the man she was currently with was not her husband. He directly challenged her departure from God's ideal for sex and marriage as a dead-end street. Yet he did not scold her for her "lifestyle." Nor did he use the Bible as a weapon against her. Instead, he saw beneath her distorted behavior to the need and emptiness that were driving it. Without a shred of "I disapprove of you" in his words or tone, Jesus told her that he could give her water that, if she would drink it, would quench her thirst forever. He was not talking about literally drinking water. He was talking about how, for years, she had tried to quench her soul's thirst with men and sex. Jesus alone could give her what five cohabitations had promised but repeatedly failed to deliver. Jesus alone could satisfy her soul's thirst with a love that stays and is stronger than death.

> Jesus, the author of all truth, beauty, and goodness, was quick to affirm expressions of truth, beauty, and goodness wherever he saw them.

As he preached the gospel to her, Jesus affirmed the Samaritan woman when nobody, including the woman herself, expected him to do so. She said to him, "'How is it that you, a Jew, ask for a drink from me, a woman of Samaria?' (For Jews have no dealings with Samaritans.)"[12] Jesus also affirmed her dignity by asking her to meet his own need for a drink of water. She had something that would be helpful to him. Jesus was not put off by the woman. He humbly received from her and offered her something in return.

The Samaritan woman is one of many examples of how Jesus affirmed people who were not on the same page with his teaching and his ethics. There was also the adulteress to whom he said, "I do not condemn you," and the prostitute whom he praised for lavishing him with a most unorthodox display of affection. Using several of the tools of her trade—her perfume, her hair, and her lips—the prostitute loved much, which proved that she had been forgiven much. When Jesus told a story to illustrate neighbor-love, he made a nonbelieving Samaritan into the heroic Christ figure. When he saw Zacchaeus, a man who had stolen from others for all of his life, he invited himself to Zacchaeus's house for a meal (*translation:* "Zacchaeus, I want to be your friend").[13]

Good Enough for Jesus, Good Enough for Us?

What does this mean for us? I think it means that if we want to follow Jesus, we have no choice but to follow him into the world and into affirming friendships with as many people as we can, including people who do not believe or behave as we do. According to Luke 15:1-2, even "sinners" flocked to Jesus daily, and he happily welcomed them, dined with them, went to parties with them, and befriended them. Secular people wanted to be near him and hear what he had to say. Jesus had a soft spot for the least and the lost, the ostracized, the moral failures, the crooks and prostitutes and lepers, the invisibles and untouchables and people on the margins, the first-century religious community's punching bags. And he was willing to be misunderstood, caricatured, and rejected for it.

Are we?

But what if we send the wrong message? What if people think we are endorsing sin? What if . . . what if . . . what if we become guilty by association? What if people start to think that we have compromised our purity and strayed from God's law? What if people start to think that we, too, have become gluttons and drunks?

Hmmm.

"The Son of Man came eating and drinking, and they say, 'Look at him! A glutton and a drunkard, a friend of tax collectors and sinners!'"[14]

Better to be lumped in with gluttons and drunks than with image-conscious Pharisees.

The closer we are to Jesus, the further we will be from sin. Likewise, the closer we are to Jesus, the closer we will be to sinners. So close that Pharisee types will assume we are guilty simply by virtue of our associations. "Jesus! What a friend for sinners! . . ."

If Jesus were a twenty-first-century American, he would not examine people's political affiliations to decide who is in and who is out. He would not tell an unmarried, cohabiting couple that they are sinning against God without welcoming the couple into his home and circle of friends. He would not talk about how a smoking or drinking habit destroys God's temple while devouring four pieces of fried chicken at a church potluck. He would not express indignation toward "greedy Wall Street people" for corporate theft as he withholds God's tithe. He would not condemn adultery or a porn addiction as being any worse than studying the Bible with the wrong motives.

Have we grown accustomed to relationally including and excluding others based on a list of spoken or unspoken "clean laws" that have no basis in Scripture? Have we grown accustomed to scolding others for certain sins while exempting ourselves from judgment over other sins that we commit daily? I am eager for more of us to respond as G. K. Chesterton once did when asked by the *London Times*, "What's wrong with the world today?" He said simply, "Dear Sir, I am."[15]

Maybe the problem with the world isn't other people. Maybe the problem with the world is us.

How many people do you know who started following Jesus because someone scolded them, disapproved of them personally, or made it clear how appalling their "lifestyle" is? I have been a Christian for more than twenty-five years and a minister for seventeen. I have never met one.

Critique without Criticism

Does this mean we should be silent about error when we see it? Should we simply "live and let live" when we see family members, friends, and neighbors exhibiting beliefs and behaviors that could harm them or others? Of course not.

May I state the obvious? If your friend is caught in an addiction, the loving (and most affirming) thing you can do is insist that he get help. If your sister or daughter is about to leave her faithful husband for another man, the loving thing to do is tell her that if she does, you will not support her decision. If your boyfriend wants to take your relationship "to the next level" and have sex with you because he loves you, the loving thing to do is set healthy boundaries and possibly end the relationship. If your boss enlists your help to hide incriminating information from shareholders or a judge, the loving thing to do is refuse to cooperate. If your child lashes out at you and demands that you buy him a toy, the loving thing to do is *not* buy the toy.

The Bible makes clear that destructive beliefs and behaviors sometimes call us to do the courageous thing—to get in one another's way and expose paths that threaten human flourishing. Sometimes this means we must critique the people that we love—and also receive critiques from them. As the proverb says, "Faithful are the wounds of a friend; profuse are the kisses of an enemy," or the psalmist, "Let a righteous man strike me—it is a kindness; let him rebuke me—it is oil for my head."[16]

Oscar Wilde said that a true friend stabs you in the front. But the "frontal stab" will eventually leave the recipient grateful, because it is done with a scalpel and not a dagger. It will be a word that heals, not a word that destroys or crushes. Why? Because an affirming *critique* always comes from the motive of restoring and building up, unlike *criticism*, which aims to harm and tear down. Paul says, "If anyone is caught in any transgression, you who are spiritual should restore him in a spirit of gentleness."[17]

Restore . . .

. . . in a spirit of gentleness.

There is no scolding in this. There is no harshness or bullying or shaming in it either. Affirming critics stand *for* and *on behalf of* one another, not against one another. They have high hopes for one another, not disdain toward one another. They are committed, covenanted allies for one another's good, not proponents for one another's harm.

Consider Yourself

Several years ago I was in a working relationship with another pastor with whom I had nothing in common except for Jesus. Our Myers-Briggs profiles were exactly opposite, as were our working styles. We had grown up in different cultures and had different outlooks on everything from politics to the finer points of doctrine to ministry philosophy. And we butted heads. A lot. To say that we were like oil and water would have been an understatement.

One evening, in an effort to work out our differences, this fellow pastor invited me out for a beer with him, and I accepted.

Two pastors walked into a bar. . . .

We had the beer together. We talked about our upbringings and our families. We shared our stories and how each of us came into a relationship with Jesus. We shared about our most heartening and heartbreaking seasons of ministry. The evening started off really well. But then all hell broke loose.

I will spare you the details, but I think it's fair to say that that evening, my fellow pastor and I got into the ugliest verbal fight of our lives. Neither of us physically struck the other, but we both went for the jugular with words. It's an ugly thing when a couple of wordsmiths use their ministerial skill as a weapon with which to rip each other to shreds. There we were for about two hours—two pastors, two disciples of Jesus, two "masters of divinity"—slicing each other apart with words and murdering each other in our hearts.

> An affirming critique always comes from the motive of restoring and building up; criticism aims to harm and tear down.

"By this all people will know that you are my disciples, *if you have love for one another.*"[18]

Pastors need Jesus too.

As I went home that evening, I felt ashamed. I wondered if I should leave the church where I served alongside this other pastor. I also wondered if I should leave the ministry entirely. What kind of pastor gets into a fight like that and talks to another human being in that manner? Forget the pastor part; what kind of *Christian* does that? I later found out that my fellow pastor went home thinking the same things about himself.

But what if, in that moment, God had us right where he wanted us?

As I continued to walk home, a quote from Bonhoeffer's *Life Together* came to mind: "Only God knows the real state of our fellowship. . . . What may appear weak and trifling to us may be great and glorious to God."[19]

The next morning there was a knock on my office door. It was the other pastor. He asked if we could talk, then he sat down and said three things I will never forget. First, he admitted humbly that though my delivery left something to be desired, many of my criticisms of him were true. He wondered if I felt the same way about his criticisms of me. I did.

Second, he said that he thought maybe God put us together because we were both like gritty pieces of sandpaper. Sandpaper is rough all around, but when you rub two pieces of sandpaper together for a while, both become smoother—not in spite of the friction, but because of it. This was his way of saying that perhaps we need each other as part of the process of becoming more like Jesus.

Then we started to talk about our offenses against each other and, one by one, asked for each other's forgiveness. The other pastor insisted on going first.

That's what Christians do when they are in their right minds. They start with themselves. They examine and address the flaws in themselves before they examine and address the flaws in others. They judge not that they not be judged. They notice and remove the logs from their own eyes so they can see clearly enough to properly notice and remove the speck from someone else's eye.[20] They critique when called for, but as they critique they are careful not to criticize.

Envision What the Other Person Could One Day Be

The third thing that the other pastor said was that he was committed from that point forward to believing Philippians 1:6, both for himself and for me. He looked me in the eye and said,

"Scott, I am sure of this, that he who began a good work in you will bring it to completion at the day of Christ Jesus." When he looked at me and saw a caterpillar, he would choose to envision the butterfly. When he looked at me and saw a single seed, he would choose to envision the forest that the seed is going to become through Christ. And he would remind himself that God loves caterpillars just as much as God loves butterflies.

From that moment, the other pastor ceased to be "the other pastor" to me. From that moment, he was my friend, a conduit of God's grace to me, a person with whom I look forward to sharing another beer in the new heaven and new earth—with no bar fights. I look forward to the day when there is nothing in either of us to critique, but only to affirm. I look forward to that day, the day of Christ Jesus, when both of us will see with clear eyes how the friction between us contributed to the smoothing of the sandpaper and to our ultimate completion in Christ.

It is not, it never has been, and it never will be a Christian's job to judge non-Christians.

I believe that God wants us to think in similar terms about our fellow human beings who are not Christians. If a family member, friend, or neighbor is at risk of stepping into harm's way or potentially harming others, the loving thing to do is step in, affirm the person, and without judgment ask the kinds of questions Jesus asked the Samaritan woman at Jacob's well.

"You say you have no husband. This is true. The man you are with now is not your husband. How is it working out for you? Are you happy? Are you experiencing fullness? Is your soul's thirst quenched and overflowing? If not, would you like to talk about living water? If you're not ready for that, it's okay. But if you're interested, I'll be right here."

As Jim Rayburn, the founder of Young Life, used to say, we

are able to speak truth to people once we have earned the right to be heard. One of the ways we do this is by realizing that it is not, it never has been, and it never will be a Christian's job to judge non-Christians. "What have I to do with judging outsiders?" Paul writes. "God judges those outside."[21] Instead, we must affirm wherever we can and critique when we must— while never being critical.

When tempted otherwise, it is always good to remember these words from James, the half brother of Jesus:

> With [the tongue] we bless our Lord and Father, and
> with it we curse people who are made in the likeness of
> God. From the same mouth come blessing and cursing.
> My brothers, these things ought not to be so.[22]

Critique when you must. Human flourishing and redemption depend on it.

Affirm whenever and wherever you can. As the likeness of God, everyone is magnificent. As an incomplete work in progress, everyone is magnificently frail.

Chapter Six

ACCOUNTABILITY OR COMPASSION?

I don't like to commit myself about Heaven and Hell—
you see, I have friends in both places.

—MARK TWAIN

I WILL NEVER FORGET A FUNERAL I ATTENDED when I was in my early thirties. The minister did the unthinkable. Instead of offering words of comfort to the mourners, the minister used his homily to talk to them—or rather, talk loudly *at* them—about eternal damnation. I do not remember the minister's exact words. But I do remember how angry his words made me feel as he spent a full ten minutes telling crestfallen, grief-stricken friends and family members that many of them, because they did not believe in Jesus, would one day burn in hell. It's not that his words were not true. It's that they were spoken in the wrong place, at the wrong time, and in the wrong tone.

Would God be okay with my feeling angry about this minister's approach? I think he would, because Jesus also got angry at this sort of thing. Although he said more about hell than most other subjects, Jesus had a very short fuse with those who appeared enthusiastic about the idea of people suffering eternally. Once, after being rejected by a village of Samaritans, Jesus' disciples asked him for permission to call fire down from heaven to destroy the Samaritans. Jesus' response was to rebuke his disciples for thinking such a harsh thing.[1] His response makes me wonder what to do with a subject like hell. On one hand, Jesus indicated that the fire of hell is an appropriate punishment for sin.[2] On the other, he got very upset with anyone suggesting that someone else should go there.

The subject of judgment can be uncomfortable and disorienting. Additionally, damage can be done when well-intentioned but deeply misguided Christians hold forth on judgment, leaving others afraid to discuss this subject in any context at all. When believers do un-Christlike things "in the name of Christ"— whether it be Jesus' disciples seeking revenge on Samaritans, a minister angrily preaching about hell in a fragile context such as a funeral, another minister blaming non-Christians for the September 11 terrorist attacks, or a church with "God hates fags" messages picketing at the funeral of a gay teenager who had been bullied to death—they make it difficult for more thoughtful, compassionate believers to raise the subject of judgment at all. Case in point: after a recent sermon I preached on the Apostles' Creed's affirmation that Jesus "will come to judge the living and the dead," several *lifelong* believers told me that mine was the first sermon that they had *ever* heard on the subject.

This should not be the case. As I mentioned above, Jesus taught more about hell than he did other, more popular subjects such as heaven and love. Everlasting torment, everlasting fire and brimstone, weeping and gnashing of teeth—these and other images were all part of his teaching. He warned repeatedly that this judgment awaits everyone who refuses his free offer of salvation by grace through faith.

Clearly, hell was an important subject to Jesus, and he thought it should be important to us, too. It is also a subject that can become for us, as it did the prophet Ezekiel, something "as sweet as honey"[3] as we consider it more thoughtfully, carefully, and biblically.

Why Judgment Makes Sense

In his lengthy volume *Being and Nothingness*, existentialist philosopher Jean-Paul Sartre talks about how threatening it is to be "under the gaze" of someone else. To illustrate the point, Sartre tells a fictitious story of a man in a park. The man, thinking he is alone, enjoys the park's lovely surroundings until he sees someone else in the distance. The man quickly becomes paranoid about the possibility that this other person might be staring at him. Then vague feelings of shame, anxiety, and desperation overcome him. The only thing he can think about is how he might escape the piercing eyes of "the Other" and the scrutiny to which he feels himself to be vulnerable. But then, much to his relief, the man discovers that the other person is in fact not another person, but a mannequin. The feeling of shame disappears and he returns to enjoying the park.[4]

Sartre's parable seeks to capture the truth about all of us—we are the fearful man in the park. We feel threatened when we are under the scrutiny, real or perceived, of others. The possibility that someone might be judging us is unnerving and is something that we want to escape as quickly as possible. We run from criticism, even constructive criticism, because we know that a single word of criticism possesses more emotional power over us than a thousand praises. Our adrenaline starts to flow, and our hearts rush immediately to fear. Have we offended? Are we in trouble? Are we about to lose a friend? Will we be attacked or condemned?

Why do our hearts go to this place? We experience this fear of exposure because part of our human condition is to feel that we are on trial. And the truth is, we *are* on trial. We *are* being held under scrutiny. The other person in the park isn't a mannequin. We *are* being judged.

Judgment from the Outside

I remember reading an interview in the *New York Times* with novelist Amy Tan, a woman who has written some wonderful, enlightening books about immigration from China and the minority experience in America. Tan was very candid in the interview about growing up with a mother who expected a lot from her. She told the interviewer that as a child she felt that she would be a huge disappointment to her mother if she did not grow up to work as a neurosurgeon during the week and a concert pianist on the weekends. She went on to describe a conversation with her mother after it was announced that her novel *The Joy Luck Club* had reached number four on the *New York Times* Best Sellers List. After hearing the good news, Tan's mother replied, "What happened? Who's No. 3 and 2 and 1?"[5]

Many people have spent large chunks of their adult lives in counselors' offices because of impossible expectations that were placed on them by others. No matter how hard these people tried, no matter how much they invested personally to measure up to the demands of a parent, a spouse, a teacher, a coach, a neighbor, a book or music or theater critic, a boss, a board, a congregation, a minister, or a mirror . . . it was never enough. They had fallen short in the eyes of their beholders. They were a disappointment to those they were so eager to please.

We have all had critics in our lives. If we're honest, we have to admit that we have also *been* the critics of others. In each instance, the one being criticized bears a burden placed there by the critic. Without a thousand praises to counter a single criticism, we can find ourselves in a fragile, defeated place. Sometimes even a thousand praises aren't enough.

Because of how deeply we are impacted by criticism, we

protect ourselves in a multitude of ways. Our defense mechanisms can be among our closest and most loyal friends; defensiveness, fits of anger, dishonesty, shifting blame, and hiding are all strategies we put to work in order to protect our fragile egos. Another self-protecting strategy is in our tendency toward perfectionism. Sadly, when we strive for perfection not only do we fail to please others, we fail to please ourselves.

Judgment from the Inside

We human beings fall short of our own expectations; we struggle every day to believe in our worth. A single criticism, an isolated bad-hair day, an insufficient grade, or an unanswered text message can undermine our sense of being loved and accepted.

In a 1991 interview with *Vanity Fair*, Madonna put this universal human struggle into words:

> All of my will has always been to conquer some horrible feeling of inadequacy. I'm always struggling with that fear. I push past one spell of it and discover myself as a special human being and then I get to another stage and think I'm mediocre and uninteresting. And I find a way to get myself out of that. Again and again. My drive in life is from this horrible fear of being mediocre. And that's always pushing me, pushing me. Because even though I've become Somebody, I still have to prove that Somebody. My struggle has never ended and it probably never will.[6]

No matter how excellent Madonna becomes in her art, her fame, and her "special humanness," somehow it will never be good enough. *"My struggle has never ended, and it probably never will."*

Madonna sheds light on a reality that is felt especially by

people who experience success. The more accomplished they have been, the more they feel pressure to accomplish even greater things. They don't need anyone to raise the bar for them, because they are always raising the bar for themselves. Success can work like an addiction—the more successes we have, the more successes we feel we must accumulate in order to keep feeling valuable—that we are, in Madonna's words, "a Somebody." We are always one breath away from failure in our own eyes.

Even if others don't put us on trial, we will put ourselves on trial. If others don't place impossible demands upon us, we will place impossible demands upon ourselves. If others don't judge us, we will become our own judges.

Made for Perfection

As part of our human nature, we act and feel as if we must convince the world and ourselves that there is nothing in us that deserves condemning. We know that we are not perfect. But there's something in all of us that still wants, even needs, to *feel* and be *seen* as perfect. To achieve this feeling, we invest large amounts of time, money, and energy into getting closer to perfection. We want the perfect persona on social media, the perfect face and body type, the perfect résumé, the perfect romance, and the perfect spirituality. We are idealists at heart. We want to live up to the demands, even the impossible ones.

But is this because we are too hard on others and too hard on ourselves? Or is it because we are too realistic? Could there be a valid reason why we are drawn to perfection?

They say that to err is human, but if to err is human, why are we, like Madonna, so easily undone by our own imperfections? Why do words like *mediocre* and *average* sound so repulsive to us? Why are we, like Amy Tan's mother, so demanding of those who would give just about anything to receive a blessing from us? As a pastor, husband, father, and friend, these questions haunt me.

Do they haunt you?

The philosopher Blaise Pascal said that we can't handle imperfection because we are from another world—and that world, unlike the world in which we currently live, is a world of perfection. "All these . . . miseries," Pascal says, "prove man's greatness. They are the miseries of a great lord, of a deposed king."[7]

What world is Pascal talking about? It's the world that began in Eden, where the man and the woman were both naked and had no shame before God, each other, or themselves. Both were completely at ease with being "under the gaze," because they were made in the image of God and were therefore miniature reflections of him "in his being, wisdom, power, holiness, justice, goodness, and truth."[8] Before they sought independence from God, Adam and Eve in the Garden were perfect people in a perfect world. And though that perfect world has temporarily been lost, according to Jesus it will one day be restored in the new heaven and the new earth, where the glory of God will light up the place and there will be no more death, mourning, crying, or pain. *There will be no more shame and judgment*, for the old order of things will have passed away, and everything will have been made new.[9] Redeemed humanity will once again reflect fully the image of God. We will once again be the crown of his creation, "a little less than God."[10] Having been made perfect again in the likeness of Jesus Christ, we will reassume the greatness and the kingliness of which Pascal speaks.

To err isn't human after all. To err is, cosmically speaking, an anomaly. That's why we can't bear the imperfection in ourselves and in others. That's why we feel on trial and why we repeatedly put others on trial. That's why we can't stand to *be* or to *appear* imperfect: we come from a perfect world. We are, as Pascal says, deposed kings who are miserable because we were created to be great.

Our human craving to be free from scrutiny, criticism, and judgment is really an echo of where history began and where history will eventually end. Both the origin of all humanity and the destiny of redeemed humanity are worlds in which there is no judgment because there is no imperfection in them.

Damning Damnation

In the last chapter of the Bible, Jesus is presented as the King whose reign of grace will never end. King Jesus assures everlasting joy and the end of scrutiny and judgment for all "who wash their robes, so that they may have the right to the tree of life and that they may enter the city by the gates."[11]

How are these robes going to be washed? I will get to that in a moment. But for now we should return to the unsettling theme of judgment—because that, too, is part of the last chapter:

> Outside are the dogs and sorcerers and the sexually immoral and murderers and idolaters, and everyone who loves and practices falsehood. . . .
>
> I warn everyone who hears the words of the prophecy of this book: if anyone adds to them, God will add to him the plagues described in this book, and if anyone takes away from the words of the book of this prophecy, God will take away his share in the tree of life and in the holy city, which are described in this book.[12]

There it is. Jesus, who promises everlasting paradise to some, also promises everlasting misery for others.

So it turns out that Sartre's man in the park *does* face the threat of "the gaze." God is not a figment of the imagination. He is not like a harmless mannequin in the park. He is a morally perfect God whose eyes are too pure to look on evil and whose presence sends even the very best people to their knees. The Old Testament prophet Isaiah, upon seeing a vision of God, pronounced woes upon himself. Why? Because in comparison to God, he realized that all the great sermons he had preached and all the good works he had done added up to nothing in terms of making him fit for the presence of God.

As with Isaiah, so it is with us. God's eyes see beneath our facades and our polished exteriors far better than we are able to see ourselves. His eyes are the eyes of "the Other"—the eyes that will find us out, call our bluff, and reckon with us at the end of time. How he chooses to reckon with us on the last day—with each and every one of us—will decide how we will spend eternity. We will either be welcomed into a life that's better than we've ever dreamed, or we will be cast out into a life that's worse than we've ever dreaded.

I'm going to state the obvious. Most people will be very uncomfortable with that last paragraph and might even decide to throw this book into the fireplace because of it. Like Charles Darwin, many of us feel this way about the explicit, damning nature of judgment:

> I can indeed hardly see how anyone ought to wish
> Christianity to be true; for if so the plain language
> of the text seems to show that the men who do not
> believe, and this would include my Father, Brother,
> and almost all my best friends, will be everlastingly
> punished. And this is a damnable doctrine.[13]

Many of us are quick to embrace the biblical doctrine of heaven but are inclined to damn the biblical doctrine of damnation. It is difficult biblical teachings like judgment that help us discern the degree to which we really do (or do not) stand with Jesus. But Jesus' invitation to follow him is an all-or-nothing proposition. Add anything to what he taught or subtract anything from what he taught, and we show ourselves to be on the outside of his circle. To damn anything that Jesus said is to damn ourselves.

Oppressing the Victims; Excusing the Oppressors

When we call the Bible's teaching about judgment into question, we not only put ourselves at risk; we also put all victims of injustice, violence, and oppression at risk. We make the vulnerable people of the world even more vulnerable, and we permit the bullies to continue bullying, by insisting that God is a God only of love, not a God of judgment.

If all people go to heaven, and if there is no ultimate accounting for evil, what are we to say to the Jews about Hitler? What are we to say to the victims of abuse? What are we to say to little girls who have been sold into the sex trade by heartless bullies who care nothing for their personhood? What are we to say to those whose lives have been confined to slavery, poverty, and oppression for no other reason but to serve the economic interests of their oppressors?

It's not as simple as saying we don't want a God who judges people. If a judging God were removed from the universe, it would create more problems than it would solve. If a judging God did not exist, then we would be living in a world of Darwinian chaos in which the strong eat the weak and only the powerful survive. For this reason, in any discussion about compassion and judgment we have to listen carefully to those who have fallen victim to injustice.

Martin Luther King Jr. once said that it is impossible to

drive out hate with more hate; only love can drive out hate. Famously, Dr. King urged his followers to resist responding to violence and oppression *with* violence and oppression. Was Dr. King saying that it is wrong to want retribution for those who oppress the disadvantaged and the weak? Of course he wasn't saying that. But he was urging his followers to leave retribution in God's hands.

Miroslav Volf, a Croatian who is very familiar with the impact of injustice on victims, believes that Dr. King's courageous ideal is impossible without an accompanying belief in a God who pledges to hold bullies accountable for their bullying. In his magnificent book *Exclusion and Embrace*, Volf says that victims' commitment to forgiveness and nonviolence requires belief in divine vengeance:

> "The only means of prohibiting all recourse to violence *by ourselves*" is to insist that violence is legitimate "only when it comes from God." . . .
>
> If God were *not angry* at injustice and deception and *did not* make the final end to violence God would not be worthy of our worship. . . . Violence thrives, secretly nourished by belief in a God who refuses to wield the sword.
>
> My thesis . . . will be unpopular with many Christians, especially theologians in the West. . . . I suggest imagining that you are delivering a lecture in a war zone. . . . Among your listeners are people whose cities and villages have been first plundered, then burned and leveled to the ground, whose daughters and sisters have been raped, whose fathers and brothers have had their throats slit. . . . The thesis: we should not retaliate since God is perfect noncoercive love. Soon you would discover that it takes the quiet of a

suburban home for the birth of the thesis that human nonviolence corresponds to God's refusal to judge. In a scorched land, soaked in the blood of the innocent, it will invariably die.[14]

Howard Thurman, a predecessor to Dr. King and an African American scholar and minister, gave a lecture at Harvard in 1947 during the pre–civil rights era. In that lecture he shared these words: "Can you imagine a slave saying, 'I and all my children and grandchildren are consigned to lives of endless brutality and grinding poverty? There's no judgment day in which any wrongdoing will ever be put right?'"[15]

Volf and Thurman are saying the same thing: if there is no final judgment, then there is really no hope for a slave, a rape victim, a child who has been abused or bullied, or people who have been slandered or robbed or had their dignity taken from them. If *nobody* is ultimately called to account for violence and oppression, then the victims will not see justice, *ever*. They will be left to conclude the same thing that Elie Wiesel concluded after the Holocaust stripped him of his mother, his father, his sister, and his faith: "I was alone, terribly alone in a world without God. . . . Without love or mercy."[16] If we insist on a universe in which there is no final reckoning for evil, this is what we are left with.

> To accept that God is a lover but not a judge is a luxury that only the privileged and protected can enjoy.

What I'm saying here is that we *need* a God who gets angry. We *need* a God who will protect his kids, who will once and for all remove the bullies and the perpetrators of evil from his playground. Those who cannot or will not appreciate this have likely enjoyed a very sheltered life and are therefore naive about the emotional impact of oppression, cruelty, and injustice. To accept that God is a lover but not a judge is a luxury that only the privileged and protected can enjoy.

God's Response to His Own Judgment: Compassion

What if I told you that the reason Jesus spoke so much about eternal fire and brimstone, weeping and gnashing of teeth, and the everlasting miseries of hell is that he loves us? What if even God agonized over the judging attribute of his character—not because it's a flawed attribute but because the thought of anyone, even his enemies, bearing the necessary burden of his judgment makes him heartsick? What if I told you that God's compassion is there and available, not only for the victims but also for the perpetrators? (King David, a murderer and a sex offender, is one of the Bible's many examples of this.) What if God's anger toward human ambivalence, injustice, toxicity, and sin is a sign that he actually *loves* us? Rebecca Pippert says this:

> We tend to be taken aback by the thought that God could be angry. . . . We take pride in our tolerance of the excesses of others. So what is God's problem? . . . But love detests what destroys the beloved. Real love stands against the deception, the lie, the sin that destroys. . . . E. H. Gifford wrote, ". . . the more a father loves his son, the more he hates in him the drunkard, the liar, the traitor." . . . Anger isn't the opposite of love. Hate is, and the final form of hate is indifference.[17]

In other words, Jesus is so vocal about wrath and judgment precisely because he loves those he is angry with. Did you know that the Bible says that God takes no pleasure in the death of anyone, even "the wicked"? Did you know that Jesus, having been rejected and persecuted by the people of Jerusalem, did not despise them but instead wept over them because of his view that they were "harassed and helpless, like sheep without a shepherd"? Did you know that Jesus, after stopping Saul of Tarsus from arresting and murdering *more* Christians, forgave Paul and turned him into history's greatest ambassador for Christianity?[18]

Jesus said so much about hell and judgment for two main reasons that I can surmise.

First, he wants us to remember that God is holy and that even the most lovely, kindhearted people among us will never measure up to that holiness. "All have sinned and fall short of the glory of God."[19] We need mercy if we are going to be spared. The truth about judgment prepares us to receive grace and forgiveness from God, which he freely offers and richly provides. Just as the prophet Isaiah found relief from judgment at the altar of mercy, having his guilt removed and his sin atoned for,[20] so believers in Jesus find relief at his cross. For those who believe in Jesus, the Cross moves their Judgment Day from the future to the past. How? Jesus already died the death that they deserved to die. Jesus already experienced the rejection, abandonment, suffering, and sorrow due to them because of their sin debt. Jesus has already been led into the dark abyss of hell so that believers, resting in his finished work alone, may now ascend to the joys of heaven. In Jesus our worst crimes of thought, word, and deed have already been punished. Through Jesus, God has no anger left for us. "There is therefore now no condemnation for those who are in Christ Jesus."[21] Thanks be to God.

The second reason why Jesus said so much about hell and judgment is that he is eager to spare us from both. He is eager to point us to life instead of death, to renewal instead of ruin, to everlasting joy instead of everlasting sorrow. He does this by pointing us to himself as the way of escape. Jesus talks so much about God's wrath because he never wants us to taste it. He tells us about the anger of God so that in being united with him through faith, we will never have to taste that anger ourselves. As a good parent speaks sharply and loudly to keep a child from running into traffic, the compassionate Jesus speaks

> For those who believe in Jesus, the Cross moves their Judgment Day from the future to the past.

sharply and loudly about judgment so we will "flee from the wrath to come"[22] as we flee into his merciful arms.

A Hard but Necessary Subject

Are there times in which it is not only appropriate, but also right and good, for Christians to tell others about the judgment of God? We must conclude that it is not the least compassionate, but the most compassionate Christians who will do so. As Rebecca Pippert says, real love *stands against* that which destroys the beloved.

So then, why would we *not* want to discuss the subject of judgment with friends and family who are not in relationship with Jesus? Why would lifelong believers say they have *never* heard a sermon about hell? Is it because we don't actually believe there will be a judgment? Is it because we want others to miss out on the safety and joy promised to those who believe? Or is it because we have a streak of codependency in us, fearing the social awkwardness that we would encounter by bringing up an uncomfortable subject?

The more threatening the cancer, the more aggressive a faithful doctor will be to get it removed. The more deadly the addiction, the more aggressive a loving family will be in confronting it. The more likely a child is to drink poison, the more aggressive a loving parent will be in screaming, "Stop!" The more distanced a friend is from God, the more direct a loving Christian will be in conversations about eternal realities.

This excerpt from Penn Jillette, an atheist illusionist and comedian, quoted in *The Atlantic*, says as much:

> I don't respect people who don't proselytize. I don't respect that at all. If you believe that there's a heaven and hell and people could be going to hell or not getting eternal life or whatever, and you think that it's not really worth telling them this because it would make it socially awkward. . . . How much do you have to hate somebody to believe that everlasting life is possible and not tell them that?[23]

How much do you have to hate somebody . . . ? Wow.

Like it or not, according to Jesus, heaven is for real . . . and so is its antithesis, hell.

The hard news is that if we really believe in a loving God, we are going to have to come to terms with this truth. If we believe in God, we are going to have to talk to the people in our lives about judgment—not in an impersonal, harsh way, but in the context of genuine friendship, with humility, thoughtfulness, love . . . and, when called for, tears.

The good news is that anyone who fears God will never have any reason to be afraid of God.

Chapter Seven

HYPOCRITE OR
WORK IN PROGRESS?

Can we only speak when we are fully living what we are saying? If all our
words had to cover all our actions, we would be doomed to permanent
silence! Sometimes we are called to proclaim God's love even when we are
not yet fully able to live it. Does that mean we are hypocrites? Only when
our own words no longer call us to conversion. Nobody completely lives up
to his or her own ideals and visions. But by proclaiming our ideals and
visions with great conviction and great humility, we may gradually grow
into the truth we speak. As long as we know that our lives always speak
louder than our words, we can trust that our words will remain humble.

—HENRI NOUWEN

"I LIKE YOUR CHRIST, I DO NOT LIKE YOUR CHRISTIANS. Your
Christians are so unlike your Christ."

These famous words attributed to Mahatma Gandhi sum-
marize one of his chief reasons for choosing Hinduism over
Christianity—for "taking sides" against Christianity while
remaining favorably disposed to Jesus. As Gandhi saw it,
Christianity was not a viable religion because it failed to impact
the lives of its adherents in any meaningful way. In comparing
Christianity to Hinduism, he said the following:

The pious lives of Christians did not give me anything
that the lives of men of other faiths had failed to give.
I had seen in other lives just the same reformation that
I had heard of among Christians. Philosophically there
was nothing extraordinary in Christian principles.
From the point of view of sacrifice, it seemed to me

that the Hindus greatly surpassed the Christians. It was impossible for me to regard Christianity as a perfect religion or the greatest of all religions.[1]

These are perplexing words for Christians to hear. For most of us, it is the "extraordinariness of Christian principles"—God moving toward us in love because Jesus sacrificed for us, not because we sacrificed for him—that makes Christian truth so appealing, so relieving, and so unique. Gandhi's words against Christianity are equally perplexing when we consider how as a Hindu, Gandhi embodied the humanitarian ethic of Jesus Christ in an exceptional fashion.

Gandhi saw very little of Christ in the lives of Christians.

An adviser to kings and nobility and having kept the company of countless celebrities, Gandhi defined himself first and foremost as a friend of the lower class. Those who were labeled by the Hindu caste system as "untouchables" were given a new name by Gandhi: "The Children of God." When asked why he rode the third-class train car with peasants and farm animals, he said it was because there was no fourth-class car. Rather than avoiding the contagion of leprosy, he personally cared for patients by bandaging and bathing them. He would not throw away a pencil until he had used it all the way down to the nub, out of respect for the person who made the pencil. When asked how far he would go to love his enemies, Gandhi replied that if an atom bomb were dropped on India, he hoped that he would look up, watch without fear, and pray for the pilot.[2]

According to Gandhi, his way of life was inspired first and foremost by the life and teachings of Jesus.[3] Yet Gandhi never seriously considered becoming a Christian.

Not because of Christ, but because of Christians.

As Gandhi observed Christians in Europe, he saw racism and self-righteousness instead of love. Once he was asked to leave a church service because he was not white, and he was routinely denied rooms and tables at Christian-owned hotels and restaurants because he was a Hindu. Gandhi saw very little of Christ in the lives of Christians.[4]

Unfortunately, Gandhi was not alone in his displeasure with the people of Jesus. Novelist Walker Percy expresses the same complaints through one of his characters in *The Second Coming*:

> I am surrounded by Christians. They are generally speaking a pleasant and agreeable lot, not noticeably different from other people—even though they . . . have killed off more people in recent centuries than all other people put together. Yet I cannot be sure they don't have the truth. But if they have the truth, why is it the case that they are repellent precisely to the degree that they embrace and advertise that truth? One might even become a Christian if there were few if any Christians around.[5]

Ouch.

This is not exactly the city on a hill Jesus envisioned Christians would be, shining as a light that all might see and glorify their Father in heaven. What are we to make of this?

I wish a case could be made that Christianity and hypocrisy are mutually exclusive, that they don't go together. But history and even the Bible tell us that they often do. The Bible itself says that we all fall short, we all do things that our inmost selves don't want to do, and even our best deeds are as filthy rags in comparison to the goodness of God.[6]

The people of Jesus are woefully unable to represent Christ as Christ represents himself. In the midst of this tension, could there be a type of "Christian hypocrite" that is less off-putting and more winsome, less offensive and more inviting, less irritating and more endearing? Is there a more "perfect imperfection" we could pursue—one about which Gandhi, if he were still with us today, might say, "I like your Christ, and I also like your Christians"?

I believe that the Bible and history both show that there is.

Christians Are Hypocrites—It's True!

When I became a Christian in my early twenties, I was an enthusiastic new convert. Jesus had brought a sense of meaning and purpose into my life. I suddenly had a new status: forgiven sinner, child of God, heir of the universe with a hope and a future. In addition to receiving these gifts, I began to feel that my life mattered, that I could make a difference, more than I ever had before. I also had unparalleled amounts of optimism about the kind of person I would become over time: less selfish and more loving, less greedy and more generous, less covetous and more content, less lazy and more disciplined, less impulsive and more responsible, less abrasive and more kind. I was confident that the Spirit's fruit of love, joy, peace, patience, kindness, goodness, faithfulness, gentleness, and self-control[7] would become such a part of me that eventually it would be difficult for people to tell the difference between Jesus and me.

Seriously?

What was I thinking?

I Am a Hypocrite

Since that time, I have grown in many ways. I am more patient and compassionate than I once was. I am also more resilient, better able to receive difficult news and go through difficult things with hope. I love money less than I used to. Most of the time, I love people more than I used to. I have more courage and a greater willingness to take risks and confront things like pride and legalism and injustice when I see them. These are all encouraging signs that God has been at work in me over the years.

Yet I struggle to fully believe and be what I deeply know I *should* believe and be. There are also areas in which I have not progressed much. In some ways, I think it is fair to say I am *worse* than I was before I became a Christian. At least, it often feels that way.

Early in my ministry I became so discouraged about my own lack of contentment, anxiety about the future, fixation on people's approval, and tendency to compare the "success" of my ministry to the ministry of others that I felt like quitting my ministry work altogether. I had not become tired of ministry. I had not become tired of God or of people. I had become tired of *myself*. I thought, *If I still have more in common with my "old self" than I do with Jesus, do I really belong in ministry? If after many years as a Christian I still struggle with some of these things, am I going to be more of a hindrance to the cause of Jesus than I am a help to the cause of Jesus? Should someone like me be a pastor?*

Then I heard Steve Brown of Key Life ministries give a talk about pastors and preaching. I don't remember anything that Steve said except for one statement, which I have held onto ever since. Steve, a seasoned minister, said that if pastors were allowed to preach only about the things that they were perfectly able to believe and practice, then they would not have anything to preach about.

The Bible Is Full of Hypocrites

It's not just modern people who struggle to live consistently with what they believe. The Bible reveals again and again the timeless tension of humanity grappling with hypocrisy.

Moses, the prophet of Israel, doubted God and resisted

God's call on his life. Abraham and Isaac, two of the three great patriarchs of Israel, both put their wives in harm's way in order to protect themselves. Jacob, the third great patriarch, was a liar. Joseph, who would later save Israel from ruin, arrogantly taunted his brothers. David, the man after God's own heart and author of most of the Psalms, committed adultery and murder. Solomon, the son of David and the wisest king of his time, was a womanizer. Rahab, a hero of the faith who protected and hid the Israelite spies, was a prostitute. Many of the great kings such as Asa and Hezekiah, who "did right in the eyes of the LORD,"[8] flirted with idolatry and finished poorly.

That's just the Old Testament.

In the New Testament, we also see plenty of hypocrisy. Thomas initially refused to believe that Jesus rose from the dead. Paul admitted to "all kinds of covetousness."[9] Peter had an abrasive personality. Peter and Barnabas fell into old patterns of elitism and exclusion, retreating relationally from their Gentile brothers and sisters. The Corinthian church, affectionately referred to by Paul as "saints" and daughters and sons of the Father, also bore some rotten fruit. They judged one another, created major divisions over minor doctrines, committed adultery, filed lawsuits against one another, had more divorces than healthy marriages, paraded their "Christian liberty" before those with a sensitive conscience, and slighted the poor, disadvantaged, and disabled in their midst.

I can allow my hypocrisy to be brought into the light by God and others.

Yikes.

I like your Christ, I do not like your Christians.

As strange as it may sound, it is the hypocrisy of Christians in the Bible that sometimes encourages me more than anything else. It reminds me that God's relentless grip on me, not my relentless grip on God, keeps me in his love. It reminds me that if there is hope for prostitutes and crooks and adulterers and racists and elitists and murderers and terrible husbands and coveters, then there is hope for somebody like me.

Another thing I appreciate about Christianity is that it gives me freedom to be honest about my sins, shortcomings, and inconsistencies. Because I have been forgiven for all my past, present, and future failures through the death and resurrection of Jesus, being found lacking is no longer a real threat, only a perceived one. The more I recognize that because of Jesus I will never have to face God's judgment, the more I can allow my hypocrisy to be brought into the light by God and others. I can also invite God and others to help me forsake my hypocrisy and grow into the person God has created me to be.

I wish that Mahatma Gandhi had seen that Christianity, in its purest and most biblical definition, is a religion that gives peace and hope and purpose to the hypocrite in all of us.

It's about Jesus

There are so many more things to affirm about Gandhi than there are things to critique. He was an exemplary and sacrificial man, a world leader for justice and peace. He never lost sight of his mission to reclaim dignity and honor for "the least of these." Gandhi behaved in more Christlike ways than many Christians ever have or will . . . including me.

But as I think about Gandhi's reasons for rejecting Christianity, I find myself asking if it is consistent to walk away from Christianity, to reject the full gospel of Christ, because of Christian hypocrisy. If Christ is the center of Christianity, then why would a person reject Christ's full message because of something more peripheral than Christ himself—namely, the inconsistency of some of his followers?

It is perfectly legitimate to have reservations about any belief system that fails to produce meaningful transformation in the lives of its followers. If I am honest, I have to admit that there are things about my own life that are not so compelling. But should my or other Christians' hypocrisy be the main reason, or any reason at all, for not following Christ? Shouldn't we evaluate Jesus on his own merits rather than the flaws of his followers?

> The hypocrite question is an important question. But is it the *main* question?

Is Jesus who he said he was? Did he really create the universe? Did he give up his life freely and voluntarily so that anyone who trusts in him can be forgiven and become a child of God? Did he rise from the dead and ascend into heaven and sit down at the right hand of God the Father Almighty? Did he treat sick people and poor people and people with regrets and moral failures with the same amount of dignity and honor that he showed to kings and queens? Is his grace greater than any sin or failure? Is he God? Is he the Savior of the universe? Is he coming again to judge the living and the dead? Is he going to make all things new? *Is he who he said he was?* Is it true that he is the Way, the Truth, and the Life and that no one comes to God except through him?

These are bigger questions than whether or not Christians are hypocrites. Don't get me wrong. The hypocrite question is an important question. But is it the *main* question?

The Russian novelist Leo Tolstoy was what many, including Tolstoy himself, would regard as a hypocritical Christian. Christian truth is an undercurrent in most of Tolstoy's acclaimed writings, but by his own admission he failed on many counts to practice the things he said he believed. To those who were prone to criticize Christianity because of Tolstoy's failures, he made this plea in a letter:

"You preach very well, but do you carry out what you preach?" This is the most natural of questions and one that is always asked of me; it is usually asked victoriously, as though it were a way of stopping my mouth. . . . And I answer that I do not preach, that I am not able to preach, although I passionately wish to. I can preach only through my actions, and my actions are vile. . . . And I answer that I am guilty, and vile, and worthy of contempt for my failure to carry them out. . . . I have failed to fulfill [Christian precepts] not because I did not wish to, but because I was unable to. Teach me how to escape from the net of temptations that surrounds me. . . . Attack *me* rather than the path I follow and which I point out to anyone who asks me where I think it lies. If I know the way home and am walking along it drunkenly, is it any less the right way because I am staggering from side to side! If it is not the right way, then show me another way.[10]

Now that we have acknowledged the "embarrassing relative" part, did you know that Jesus also has some lovely relatives?

Imperfect Reflections

Even though all fall short, there is still a lot of truth, beauty, and goodness that come into the world through the people of Jesus. None reflect Christ perfectly, but many reflect him still.

King David, for example, fell into deep hypocrisy when he slept with another man's wife and then arranged for the man to be killed in battle. But there is more to the David story. When Nathan the prophet came and confronted David for these things, David was cut to the heart and openly confessed and humbly accepted the consequences for the wrongs he had done, taking full responsibility for his actions. Before and after his season of backsliding and shame, David was loyal, faithful, courageous, humble, broken, and benevolent . . . and he gave us most of the Psalms.

There are many other Christians like David who, though inconsistent and hypocritical in certain areas and seasons of their lives, have brought unparalleled goodness and beauty into the world in response to the grace and love of Christ.

In one of his op-ed columns in the *New York Times*, journalist Nicholas Kristof makes the following observation about evangelical Christians:

> Some [self-appointed evangelical leaders] seem homophobic, and many who claim to be "pro-life" seem little concerned with human life post-uterus. Those are the preachers who won headlines and disdain. But in reporting on poverty, disease and oppression, I've seen so many others. Evangelicals are disproportionately likely to donate 10 percent of their incomes to charities. . . . More important, go to the front lines, at home or abroad, in the battles against hunger, malaria, prison rape, obstetric fistula, human trafficking or genocide, and some of the bravest people you meet are evangelical Christians . . . who truly live their faith. *I'm not particularly religious myself,* but I stand in awe of those I've seen risking their lives in this way—and it sickens me to see that faith mocked at New York cocktail parties.[11]

In spite of the inconsistencies of people like Abraham, Isaac, Jacob, Peter, Paul, and Tolstoy, no other religion, philosophy, or person has inspired self-donating love and sacrificial service more than a vital, living faith in Jesus Christ and the power of his death and resurrection. It is through imperfect Christians that scores of life-giving contributions have left the world better, not worse—and about which even Gandhi might be inspired.

Numerous Christians, moved by the order and magnificence of the Creator's creation, have made game-changing contributions to the world of science and mathematics. Francis Collins (the genome project), Blaise Pascal (statistics), Copernicus (the heliocentric theory), and Isaac Newton (calculus), to name just a few, pursued scientific inquiry not in spite of their faith but because of it.

Other Christians, moved by Jesus' mission to heal and restore, have been responsible for significant progress in the world of health care. Have you ever noticed how many hospital titles begin with the word "Saint" because they were founded and funded by followers of Jesus? Did you know that Dr. C. Everett Koop, a devoted Christian and surgeon general of the United States when the AIDS epidemic first broke in the gay community, was the world's foremost leader in fighting this horrible disease?

Others, moved by the beauty and creativity of God, have produced groundbreaking works of art. World-class painters such as Rembrandt, world-class musicians such as Beethoven and Haydn and Johnny Cash and Bono, and world-class writers such as Dostoevsky and T. S. Eliot, to name a few, credit their creative genius to Jesus.

There are many other examples.

Christians are, by and large, significantly different from many of the negative caricatures sometimes portrayed in media, comedy, and film. Most of us, when we act out of sync with the life, teachings, and mission of Jesus, are actually not proud of it but grieved by it. Like Tolstoy, most of us want to be better than we are and don't want to live as hypocrites. Most of us are our own worst critics. It's true. Though we are at times offensive and insensitive, and Jesus could easily sue us for defamation of character if he wanted to, most of us *want* our lives to be a demonstration of who Jesus is and what Jesus is like. We have seasons and spurts in which Jesus is pleased to show the world who he is and what he is like, not in spite of us, but through us. This is why, as a Christian, I appreciate when non-Christians like Nicholas Kristof of the *New York Times* are willing to speak not only of the unsavory things but also of the good and beautiful things that Jesus is doing through his people. The creator and host of *This American Life*, Ira Glass, is another non-Christian whose balanced, kindhearted perspective I appreciate:

> What Christians *really are* is not being captured by the press. . . . I feel that Christians are really horribly covered by the media. . . . And there came a point early on in the show that I just noticed that the way that Christians are portrayed in movies and on television is almost always as these crazy people. . . . Where as the Christians in my life were all incredibly wonderful and thoughtful and had very ambiguous, complicated feelings in their beliefs. And seemed to be totally generous-hearted—totally opened to a lot of different kinds of people in their lives.[12]

The Authentic Hypocrite

I am eager for my non-Christian friends to see that even for hypocrites, there is a hope and beauty that comes through Christ. I am eager for my non-Christian friends to see that yes, we Christians sometimes live inconsistently with what we believe . . . and we will continue to do so (albeit, inadvertently) until we die or until Jesus returns and makes everything, including us, new again. I am also eager for my fellow Christians to feel okay about owning this fact, and to admit our failures publicly and winsomely and often. It's time we learned from GK Chesterton: "What's wrong with the world? I am."

I dream of a day, hopefully soon, when Gandhi sympathizers will begin saying, "I like your Christ *and* I like your Christians," not because we Christians have ceased to be hypocrites, but because we have become increasingly endearing *in* and honest and sad *about* our hypocrisy. There is something incredibly attractive and inviting about people who stop pointing fingers and posing and pretending to be totally good and totally right, and instead start taking themselves less seriously and openly and freely admit that they are not yet what they should be. I am eager for the Christian story to put a spotlight on the same thing that the biblical story does—that Jesus is quite fond of humbled hypocrites, and he loves to save humbled hypocrites from themselves.

But there is more.

Tolstoy was partly right and partly wrong. He was right in saying that it's the integrity of the path he follows, not the way in which he drunkenly stumbles along it, that deserves the fullest consideration. But Tolstoy was wrong in saying that he is unable to find an escape from the temptations that surround him. This is why Paul wrote these words to a church filled with hypocrites:

No temptation has overtaken you that is not common to man. God is faithful, and he will not let you be tempted beyond your ability, but with the temptation he will also provide the way of escape, that you may be able to endure it. Therefore, my beloved, flee from idolatry. . . . Whether you eat or drink, or whatever you do, do all to the glory of God. . . . Be imitators of me, as I am of Christ.[13]

A Way of Escape for Those Who Are Tired of Their Own Hypocrisy

Though we are all hypocrites, through Christ and with Christ and because of Christ we are never hopelessly and terminally *stuck* in our hypocrisy. A central focus of the vision of Jesus is to save us from sin—and in the process, to save us from ourselves.

But in saving us from ourselves, Jesus also aims to transform us, over time, into his own likeness.

I love how Anne Lamott said that it's okay to realize you're very crazy and very damaged, because all of the best people are.[14] I love this because it is in seeing and owning that we are crazy and damaged, it is in crying "uncle" to our failed self-reformation projects, it is in recognizing that we are most certainly "so unlike our Christ"—that Christ begins to change us. It is when we become tired of ourselves, weary of our own failed efforts, that Jesus meets us with hope.

But how does he meet us? How are we actually changed? How does Jesus transform our selfishness into servanthood, our greed into generosity, our dishonesty into truthfulness, our ugliness into beauty, our hypocrisy into holiness?

Furthermore, how does the loveliness of Jesus become *recognizable* in us? How do family and friends and neighbors and colleagues become more intrigued by Jesus—in spite of the hypocrisy they see in us—because of an irresistible truth, beauty, and love *resembling Jesus* that they see growing in us as well? How does the Tolstoy in all of us get unstuck and find a way to "escape from the net of temptations that surrounds" us and move toward being the city on a hill, the light in dark places, and the salt of the earth that Jesus envisioned? How do we Christians, even with our inconsistencies

> Only the loveliness of Jesus can make hypocrites lovely.

and shortcomings, become the kind of people who make others want to know more about Jesus?

The Bible helps us see how: it is the loveliness of Jesus, and only the loveliness of Jesus, that can make hypocrites lovely.

To grumpy and elitist Christian hypocrites in Galatia, Paul writes:

> The fruit of the Spirit is love, joy, peace, patience, kindness, goodness, faithfulness, gentleness, self-control. . . . Those who belong to Christ Jesus have crucified the flesh with its passions and desires.[15]

To immoral and divisive Christian hypocrites in Corinth, Paul writes:

> Do you not know that the unrighteous will not inherit the kingdom of God? Do not be deceived: neither the sexually immoral, nor idolaters, nor adulterers, nor men who practice homosexuality, nor thieves, nor the greedy, nor drunkards, nor revilers, nor swindlers will inherit the kingdom of God. And such were some of you. But you were washed, you were sanctified, you were justified in the name of the Lord Jesus Christ and by the Spirit of our God.[16]

Noting the transformation that had occurred in Peter and John, Luke the Evangelist writes:

> When [the rulers, scribes, and religious leaders] saw the boldness of Peter and John, and perceived that they were uneducated, common men, they were astonished. And they recognized that they had been with Jesus.[17]

How do hypocrites become *like* Jesus? It starts by belonging *to* Jesus, by being washed, sanctified, and justified *by* Jesus, and especially by being *with* Jesus.

One of my favorite moments in ministry occurred during a Saturday-evening wedding reception. The best man, also the brother of the groom, stood up to give his toast. Spoons rattled against the water glasses, eyes turned toward the front, and he said to his brother, in front of everyone,

> It's no secret to anyone here that I have never liked you. All of our lives we have fought and argued and have been like oil and water. We are still very different in many ways. But I have grown to love the person you have become since the day you met *her*. The more you are with *her*, the more I am drawn to you. The more you are with *her*, the more I want to be around you. The more you are with *her*, the more I see in you the best version of yourself.

There was an awkwardness as well as a sweetness to this toast. But its sweetness is what has made the most indelible impression on me ever since, because it is such a profound picture of how Jesus changes his people. Just as being with his bride brought out the very best in the groom, being with Jesus brings out the best in us. And the more we are with him, the more everyone around us, including "estranged brothers," starts to feel the impact of transformation.

It is in belonging *to* Jesus, it is in being washed, sanctified, and justified *by* Jesus, it is in being *with* Jesus that hypocrites start to become *like* Jesus. Bullies become kind, elitists become approachable, adulterers become pure, takers become givers, narcissists become servants, haters become lovers, adversaries become advocates, sinners become saintly, and hypocrites become winsome even as they continue to wrestle with their own shortcomings.

Humbled by our own hypocrisy and drawn to how the loveliness of Jesus can transform us, we must preoccupy ourselves less with trying to be like him and more with simply being with him . . . because the closer we are to Jesus, the more we yield and surrender to the light he has already put in us by his Spirit and the further we will be from selfishness and sin. The more we sit at his feet, consider his loveliness, take in his truth, breathe in his air, live in community with his people, celebrate his sacraments, and follow him in his mission, the more his aroma will be discernible in us.

As was the case for the groom, so it is the case with us. Loveliness, or holiness, or the fruit of the Spirit, or whatever we are going to call it, will not grow in us when we seek it directly. It is not fruit we should be seeking; it is Jesus. Loveliness and holiness and fruit will not grow when we *try* to make them grow. Rather, these will grow as by-products of being in the presence of, considering the excellencies of, and marinating in the truth and beauty of the one who loves us and gave himself for us and in whom there is never a shred of hypocrisy.

> It is in belonging *to* Jesus, it is in being washed, sanctified, and justified *by* Jesus, it is in being *with* Jesus that hypocrites start to become *like* Jesus.

So the next time we hear somebody say, "I like your Christ, but I do not like your Christians. Your Christians are so unlike your Christ," let's start by owning it. We are not yet what we are meant to be. We are incomplete works in progress.

But by the grace of God, let's continue to make progress. Let's aspire, as Paul called the Corinthians to aspire, to follow his example as he followed the example of Christ[18]—with full recognition that the only way to follow his example, the only way to walk away from our hypocrisy and toward Jesus, is to see and savor the fact that Jesus has already run toward us.

And as we do this, perhaps those around us will look at us and say, "I have grown to love the person you have become since the day you met *him.*"

Chapter Eight

CHASTITY OR
SEXUAL FREEDOM?

*What if the church were full of people who were loving and safe, willing to
walk alongside people who struggle? What if there were people in the church
who kept confidences, who took the time to be Jesus to those who struggle
with homosexuality? What if the church were what God intended it to be?*
—AN ANONYMOUS, SAME-SEX-ATTRACTED CHRISTIAN

ONE SUNDAY AFTER A CHURCH SERVICE, a young woman intro-
duced herself to me as a first-time visitor. After the usual "Nice
to meet you; how did you hear about our church?" conversation,
the woman wanted to know if she could ask me a direct question.
"Of course," I said. "Fire away."

Before getting to her question, she offered a short speech.
She said that she was single, sexually active, and frustrated with
Christians who, according to her, were culturally regressive on
the subject of sex. "We don't live in *Leave It to Beaver* land anymore," she continued. "I have gay and straight friends, including many who are not married, who like to have sex, and who
feel fine about it. In today's society, my friends and I are not
alone. If churches want to stay relevant, if they want to reach
the modern person, churches will need to catch up with the
world on the subject of sex."

She never asked her question.

Not too many weeks following this encounter, the *New York Times* came out with a piece about the hookup culture at Harvard University called "Students of Virginity." In the article, a student who values sexual experimentation and having sexual encounters with multiple partners summarizes her viewpoint:

> For me, being a strong woman means not being ashamed that I like to have sex. . . . To say that I have to care about every person I have sex with is an unreasonable expectation. It feels good! It feels good![1]

These are just two examples that indicate how the tide has shifted in Western culture on the subject of sexuality. Whether it is *Saturday Night Live* teasing Jimmy Carter for confessing that he lusts sometimes; Woody Allen flippantly saying, "The heart wants what the heart wants" when pressed about his affair with his teenage stepdaughter; or sex-advice columnist Dan Savage advocating for open marriages because he thinks it's unreasonable to expect people to be monogamous,[2] all indications are that, indeed, we are not in *Leave It to Beaver* land.

Historic Christianity, Judaism, Islam, and many other major world religions have always believed that God gave us sex for two reasons. First, sex is for procreation. The only way for new life to be formed is through the uniting of sperm and egg. Second, sex is a way for men and women, specifically husbands and wives, to give and receive pleasure through the uniting of two bodies into one. The one-flesh union renews and solidifies marriage vows. It serves as a reminder that husbands and wives are no longer independent but belong to each other, body and soul. The union of two naked bodies affirms every other form of nakedness—personal, emotional, and spiritual.

Yet negative reactions to the biblical vision for sex abound in modern Western society. The blogosphere and general public conversation reflect a variety of opinions on the subject of marriage and sexuality. Even within communities of faith, intramural debates and divisions abound over this single, heated issue. Is the "sex is only for marriage between one man and one woman" view too limiting? Worse, is it insensitive, unloving, and oppressive because of how it prohibits consenting adults who love one another—single, gay, straight, monogamous, and polygamous—from enjoying the same freedoms that husbands and wives do?

The church visitor's *Leave It to Beaver* comment made me wonder if she was familiar at all with the biblical vision for sex. Neither the modern hookup nor the *Leave It to Beaver* culture reflects a biblical view of sexuality. Instead, the Bible puts forward a vision for sexuality that is both chaste and free.

God Is in Favor of Chastity

Modern people often agree that as long as there are two (or more) willing parties, there really shouldn't be an issue when it comes to a more open or "adventurous" approach to sexuality. So why does God make such a big deal about sex? Why would he spoil the pleasures of variety and experimentation by limiting sex to marriage between just one man and one woman? When there is mutual consent, nobody gets hurt. *It feels good! It feels good!*

A warm fire also feels good, until we stop recognizing that it can hurt us. Like fire, sex can be incredibly life giving, comforting, and healing when handled with care. It is among the most delightful of all human activities. It is also among the most dangerous. Like fire, when sex is taken outside its natural and created boundaries, it becomes destructive, leaving burn marks and scars. That's why God is in favor of chastity, or sexual abstinence, for those living outside the covenant of marriage.[3]

Consider the current impact of pornography. According to

Frank Rich of the *New York Times*, in 2001 Americans spent between $10 billion and $14 billion each year on pornography. Current statistics indicate that US spending on pornography is still hovering around $14 billion. Additionally, a staggering $97 billion per year is spent on pornography worldwide, which means that the annual revenue for porn exceeds the revenues of the world's top technology companies combined: Microsoft, Google, Amazon, eBay, Yahoo!, Apple, Netflix, and Earthlink.[4] Frank Rich also contends that pornography as an industry has outgrown all major league sports and possibly even the Hollywood film industry. Porn is "no longer a sideshow to the mainstream," he says. "It is the mainstream."[5] The psychological and physiological impact has been devastating.

In a featured article in *New York Magazine*, Naomi Wolf observes:

> Pornography works in the most basic of ways on the brain. . . . If you associate orgasm with your wife, a kiss, a scent, a body, that is what, over time, will turn you on; if you open your focus to an endless stream of ever-more-transgressive images of cybersex slaves, that is what it will take to turn you on. The ubiquity of sexual images does not free eros but dilutes it.[6]

Gary Brooks says the following about "soft-core" pornography:

> Softcore pornography has a very negative effect. . . . Its voyeurism . . . teaches men to view women as objects rather than to be in relationships with women as human beings. . . . Pornography gives men the false impression that sex and pleasure are entirely divorced from relationships. . . . Pornography is inherently self-centered—something a man does by himself,

for himself—by using other women as the means to pleasure, as yet another product to consume.[7]

Consumers of pornography are not the only ones affected. The objectification of both men and women has transformed the way many people measure their own attractiveness. For example, nowadays it is common for a beautiful woman to have no concept of her beauty. She feels pressure to measure up to the airbrushed images she sees in magazines. She exhausts herself by undereating and overexercising, paralyzed by shame because she cannot fit into a size two. How will she ever compete with the hard-core porn goddesses on pay-per-view and the Internet, or the soft-core porn goddesses on network television and in the Victoria's Secret catalogs? I will never forget hearing the actress Kirstie Alley comment on pictures of herself, saying that she saw herself as "hideous" and "disgusting," contending that being overweight makes "you loathe yourself."[8] This is tragic, and a deception of the highest order.

What we need is a culture of true progressives who affirm the dignity and beauty of *all* women, not just the skinny and sexy few. We would be wise to stop deifying the Victoria's Secret and *GQ* bodies and rethink the meaning of "sexy." Biblically, the most interesting and attractive women and men are those whose hearts are at rest because they know that God loves them. Their beauty is from inside and is not fixated on cosmetic perfection, but on substantive character, driven by a reciprocal love for God that also frees them to love their neighbor.

A strong case can be made that casual sex and objectification—self-centered lust for people in general versus self-giving love for one person in particular—are chief contributors to unparalleled divorce rates, sexually transmitted diseases, unplanned pregnancies, body-image depression, teen suicides, terminations of life in the womb, and little girls being trafficked and sold into prostitution. Our culture of casual sex has led to outcomes that are anything but casual. Until we learn to see people as *people* instead of things, as image bearers to be loved instead of objects to be used, sexuality will only become more confused and broken.

God Is in Favor of Sexual Freedom

God puts protective boundaries around sexuality just as good parents give their children protective boundaries. Our heavenly Father does not want us to hurt ourselves. However, it is unhelpful to become reactionaries and swing the pendulum to Ward and June Cleaver of *Leave It to Beaver*, who slept in separate beds, more like college roommates than husband and wife.

> Our culture of casual sex has led to outcomes that are anything but casual.

Some people are surprised when they find out that the Bible promotes and even commands sexual pleasure. God is in favor of sexual freedom—within the bounds of marriage, as we saw earlier. In the earliest chapters of Genesis we see God creating sex and *commanding* Adam and Eve to fully enjoy each other's naked bodies: "A man shall leave his father and his mother and hold fast to his wife, and they shall become one flesh. And the man and his wife were both naked and were not ashamed."[9] The theme is continued in Proverbs, where husbands are told, "Drink water from your own cistern. . . . Rejoice in the wife of your youth. . . . Let her breasts fill you at all times with delight; be intoxicated always in her love."[10] Song of Solomon consists of eight erotic chapters in which a husband and wife sing and recite poetry about each other's naked bodies while playfully scheming about how they are going to ravish each other. God, who inspired the writing of Song of Solomon, smiles from heaven at this. Paul, inspired by the Holy Spirit, invites and even commands spouses to freely give their bodies to each other and to do so often.[11] What kind of God would command such a thing? Yet this is precisely what the biblical God does. Anyone who thinks the Bible is stuffy about sex either hasn't read the Bible or hasn't been paying attention to what it says.

People who understand the Bible's vision for sex also understand that the physical union of a man and a woman is more a sign than it is a destination. It is not an end in itself. Sex is symbolic as much as it is real. It represents a holistic approach to nakedness, full and reciprocal transparency in which man and woman are fully exposed yet not rejected, fully known yet completely embraced.

Sex also signifies our nakedness before God. Having been united with Christ, believers live in the awareness that God knows everything about us—warts and scars and all—and still loves us. God knows our secrets, the skeletons we hide in the closet, the things we are most ashamed of. He is fully aware of our worst qualities, yet tenderly says to us, "I will betroth you to me forever"[12] and, "As the bridegroom rejoices over the bride, so shall your God rejoice over you."[13] Through Christ, God carries us back to Eden where we are naked without shame, where we are received and cherished as a bride beautifully dressed for her husband on her wedding day. Sex between a husband and wife points to this ultimate union: the union between Christ and his bride, the church. It also points to the wedding feast promised to believers in the new heaven and new earth as well as the "happily ever after" we will enjoy with Jesus the Bridegroom.[14]

> Anyone who thinks the Bible is stuffy about sex either hasn't read the Bible or hasn't been paying attention to what it says.

Homosexuality—Yes, No, or Maybe?

In recent years in the West, there has been a growing movement supporting monogamous, committed same-sex relationships. Even within Christianity, some wish to revisit the long-held Christian (as well as Jewish, Muslim, and Hindu) belief that marriage and sex are for one man and one woman only. Is it fair to say that only heterosexual couples can enjoy God's gift of sexual intimacy and lifelong partnership? Have we been reading the Bible wrongly on this issue for all these years? People used to think that the Bible was pro-slavery and oppressive to women. But now, after more careful study of the Bible on these matters, we know that the opposite is true. Is homosexuality a similar issue? Is it time for a reformation? Self-identified "gay-affirming evangelicals" such as Jay Bakker, Justin Lee, Rachel Held Evans, and Matthew Vines are suggesting in their books, blogs, and Twitter posts that it is. Many are listening, and many are convinced.

There are also those who, based on a careful reading of the entire Bible, remain opposed to eroticizing same-sex relationships inside the church.

I recently told a gay Christian friend that, sadly, I was not able to affirm his romantic involvement with the man he calls "the love of his life." This was incredibly painful to do, but when a friend asks a direct question, one must answer it truthfully. I spoke from a place of grief and sadness because I want my friend to enjoy deep companionship and intimacy.

Thankfully, my friend was kind enough to listen to my reasoning as both of us held back tears. I think he is still processing what I said to him, which was this:

To affirm his union with the love of his life would mean I'd have to deny the love of mine.

The German pastor and theologian Dietrich Bonhoeffer, martyred by the Hitler regime, said that "when Christ calls a man, he bids him come and die."[15] Christ, the love of my life, bids me come and die. He bids me to have and to hold him for better or for worse, in sickness and in health, in joy and in sorrow, forsaking all others, for as long as I live and into eternity.

Jesus says that anyone "who does not renounce all that he has cannot be my disciple."[16] I am irresistibly drawn to him. I must be his disciple. So I must renounce all that contradicts him and that contradicts things that he has clearly said. But it's hard. Sometimes it puts me in a position that grieves me.

I grieve because I *want* my friend to be able to share life and be romantically involved with another person. I do not want him to be lonely or alone. Yet as a Christian I am bound to yield my personal feelings and wishes to the sacred words of Jesus, who affirmed that in the beginning, God made them male and female, and the man was united to the woman, and the two became one flesh.[17]

As the biblical proverb says, "There is a way that seems right to a man, but its end is the way to death."[18] In both the Old and New Testaments, all the direct references to homosexuality echo this proverb with a tone of sober warning, with no affirmations to counter them.[19]

The issue of slavery, often cited as an apples-to-apples comparison to homosexuality, is actually an apples-to-oranges comparison. The Bible itself was a chief reason for the abolition of slavery. Texts such as Galatians 3:28 and Paul's letter to Philemon (a first-century slave owner) put a spotlight on centuries of flawed, self-serving biblical interpretation. Here, Paul insists that as a Christian, Philemon must begin treating his servant, Onesimus, with the highest esteem—*no longer as a slave but as a brother and an equal.*[20] According to Bible scholar F. F. Bruce, Paul's New Testament letters "bring us into an atmosphere in which the institution [of slavery] could only wilt and die."[21] History has proven Bruce correct, with abolitionists and civil rights leaders such as William Wilberforce, Abraham Lincoln, and Martin Luther King Jr. opposing racism and slavery not in spite of their belief in the Bible, but because of it.

Though there is still progress to be made, similar gains have occurred on the matter of women's equality. Based on Jesus' treatment of women and the many passages in both the Old and New Testaments that elevate the dignity of women, one simply cannot make a biblical case for women being inferior to men.

Injustices such as slavery and the oppression of women have been fought against in most developed nations, largely due to a strong scriptural counter-voice that puts flawed interpretations to rest. Yet no such counter-voice can be found in the Bible that suggests a favorable view of homosexuality. For people like me who have same-sex-attracted friends, and especially for my same-sex-attracted friends themselves, this can create layers of difficulty and grief and loss and sadness. And yet the God of all comfort promises to meet us and abide with us precisely in those places. He does not invite us to censor what he has said. But he does invite us to find rest in the good that we cannot see.

This is not easy.

Some may say to a same-sex-attracted person, "Aren't we all challenged by scriptural truths that confront our deepest desires? What makes same-sex attraction such a unique struggle? Why can't you just accept this as your cross to bear, your unique calling from God, to remain single and celibate?" Asking this sort of question in this sort of way fails to appreciate the depth of a same-sex-attracted Christian's struggle. When I was a single man and had no romantic options and wanted so much to be united to a woman, surrendering to Jesus meant remaining celibate . . . for a time. Even though abstinence and purity were difficult, there was always the *possibility* of uniting my life with someone else's. No such prospect exists for a same-sex-attracted

Christian, whose surrender to Jesus truly feels like a form of death, a lover's version of Gethsemane. If I am going to have anything meaningful to contribute to this discussion, it must begin with a recognition that temporary celibacy pales in comparison with what many same-sex-attracted people feel is a lifelong prison sentence of suppressing libido and romantic feelings. For those who are not same-sex attracted, this conversation needs to begin with compassion and maintain compassion as its foundation. We must never presume to understand what it is like to walk in shoes we will never wear.

Yet the Scriptures remain, and the truth remains. All children of God, Jesus says, must deny themselves daily, take up their crosses, and follow him.[22] Some people's crosses are much weightier than others', but all must bear a cross. In my world, the lesser crosses include my inclination to worry and my anxiety-based insomnia, both of which contradict God's invitation to trust him. There is also my greed, which contradicts God's promise to fulfill my every need. And there is my craving for people's approval (even as I write this, I am fearful of how my gay and gay-affirming friends will receive it), which contradicts the favor that God has freely given me in Christ.

But God did not create me to live this way. He did not create me to accept the invitation that these confusing and broken impulses, instincts, and desires extend to me. Rather, he extends to me a different invitation: to surrender all my impulses, instincts, and desires to his lordship. Rather than entertain the idea that God created me to be fearful, greedy, and emotionally needy, he invites me to the higher ground of trusting him—trusting that his thoughts are higher than my thoughts, that his ways are higher than my ways, and that his wisdom is higher than my desires and longings. He invites me to trust that it will someday all make sense, this surrendering business, when Jesus returns to make all things new and to redeem all things confusing and broken—including my confusing and broken desires.

None of my struggles compares in weight to that of a gay man or woman surrendering all romantic longings to Jesus. I have known several gay men and women to make that surrender. I also know several same-sex-attracted people who are faithfully married to members of the opposite sex, and for whom such faithfulness is a regular but noble struggle. I am currently pastor to several of these men and women. For many of them, the surrender was heartbreaking. But it is a surrender that each of them has considered worthwhile, not because Jesus is a roadblock to love but because Jesus is love itself.

> Jesus invites us to trust that it will someday all make sense, this surrendering business.

In addition, there are others in my life who have remained *married* and *celibate* for similar reasons. These people have chosen to remain true to spouses who are relationally difficult, to spouses who have sustained a brain injury or have Alzheimer's, to spouses who are paralyzed from the neck or waist down, to spouses who are no longer physically able to have intercourse. Some of these friends are very young and are facing unique emotional, relational, and romantic challenges for the rest of their lives. And they are doing so not because Jesus is a roadblock to love but because Jesus is love itself. According to their own testimonies, these men and women have found in Jesus a love more sure, solid, enduring, and safe than any other love that would presume to compete with him.

It Is Not Good to Be Alone

If Christians are going to call their fellow Christians to heterosexual monogamy within marriage and celibacy outside of it, we must not stop there. It is necessary to go further to ensure that those who heed Jesus' sexual ethic have the support not only to succeed but also to thrive. It is not enough to say that sex outside of marriage is wrong or that erotic same-sex relationships are off limits for those who wish to follow Jesus. "The Bible says it; that settles it" is a lazy and unthoughtful approach that alienates people who long for companionship yet bear the burden of unwanted singleness and celibacy.

Jesus said, "The scribes and the Pharisees sit on Moses' seat. . . . They preach, but do not practice. They tie up heavy burdens, hard to bear, and lay them on people's shoulders, but they themselves are not willing to move them with their finger."[23] Those who are serious about following Jesus must do more than lift a finger to alleviate the burden of aloneness in our midst. Every person—married or unmarried—must have people in their lives for support, companionship, intimacy, and human touch. We must ask the radical question of what it will take to ensure that every unmarried person has access to friendships as deep and lasting as marriage and as meaningful as sex. We must also ask what it will take for our communities to effectively cultivate such friendships.

> "The Bible says it; that settles it" is a lazy and unthoughtful approach that alienates people who long for companionship yet bear the burden of unwanted singleness and celibacy.

As meaningful as sex? Seriously?

Yes, I really mean that. Have you read about David and Jonathan?

Friendship as Deep as Marriage, Community as Deep as Family

Centuries before Jesus and Paul, David and Jonathan shared a friendship that was so deep that David said, "My brother

Jonathan; very pleasant have you been to me; your love to me was extraordinary, surpassing the love of women."[24]

Some, in an effort to defend homosexuality with the Bible, have taken this single statement from David to mean that he and Jonathan were gay lovers. There is no evidence in the Bible that suggests an erotic connection. But there *is* evidence of a friendship as deep and committed as that of a married couple.

We are told that Jonathan's and David's souls were "knit together," that each loved the other as his own soul.[25] The two made a lasting covenant to always be there for each other, to have each other's backs, and even to raise each other's children should the need arise. Just as Ruth refused to leave Naomi's side, John leaned heavily into Jesus' bosom, and Jesus promised to never leave or forsake us, David and Jonathan's friendship was intimate and enduring. Their love for each other was neither marital nor sexual. Instead of naked bodies, they had naked souls.[26]

This kind of "soul-knitting" friendship, while it does not include the pleasures of erotic love, does provide strength, solace, and permanence for unmarried people, whether male or female, gay or straight, divorced or widowed or never married. W. H. Auden, a gay man who remained unmarried and celibate out of obedience to Jesus, illustrates this truth in an excerpt from a letter he wrote to a friend, about his friends:

> There are days when the knowledge that there will never be a place which I can call home, that there will never be a person with whom I shall be one flesh, seems more than I can bear, and if it wasn't for you, and a few—how few—like you, I don't think I could.[27]

What if the church became the first place, instead of the last place, that people went looking for this kind of friendship? What if the church were filled with unmarried people but had no "single" people, because married *and* unmarried people were as family to one another—surrogate brothers and sisters and mothers and fathers and sons and daughters to the rest of the church? What if the church were the place where people discovered that being unmarried is not a prison sentence but an opportunity for grace and communion with Jesus and service to God's Kingdom and mission? What if the church were the place where being unmarried was not only accepted, but seen as a high and noble calling as it was for Jesus and Paul? What if it is true that God sets the lonely in families? What if it is true that "there is no one who has left house or brothers or sisters or mother or father or children or lands, for [Jesus'] sake and for the gospel, who will not receive a hundredfold now in this time, houses and brothers and sisters and mothers and children and lands"? What if the church were the place where anyone in the world could find refuge and solace from the age-old malediction that to be alone is to be lonely?[28]

This is exactly what God intends the church to be.

Jesus Christ—Single, Celibate, Sufficient—and the Point of Marriage

There are other "what ifs" to be considered. What if the main reason God created marriage and sex is *not* so we could be married and have sex? What if God has something bigger and more ultimate in mind—something that is accessible to all people, regardless of their marital status?

He does.

Have you ever wondered why Jesus chose to be single and celibate? Could it be that he was saving himself . . . for us?

A deeper look into the full biblical narrative tells a bigger story about marriage than marriage itself. According to Paul, marriage is not a be-all and end-all, but a pointer to something bigger than marriage. "This mystery [of marriage] is profound," Paul says, "and I am saying that it refers to Christ and the church."[29]

Paul is saying that God's design for marriage is that it is preparatory and temporary. The first and fundamental goal in marriage is for a husband and wife to prepare each other for an everlasting marriage to Jesus.[30] The only marriage that will remain in the new heaven and new earth is the marriage between Jesus and his bride, the church.[31]

What does this mean? It means that whether married, unmarried, divorced, or widowed now, every believer in Jesus is and will be united with him forever in *the* marriage that will fulfill every unsatisfied longing, every unfulfilled attraction, every missed opportunity for companionship, love, and intimacy.

As Paul says, this is all a profound mystery. But we do know that even the best day of marriage in this life will pale in comparison to the worst day of marriage to Jesus in the new heaven and new earth (as if there could be a worst day). The best sex in this life will seem boring compared to the intimacy that will be enjoyed daily between Jesus and his people.

And there's more: our deepest aches, longings, and loneliness will be satisfied once Jesus sweeps up his bride into his everlasting arms.

In the meantime, will Jesus be enough for us here and now? Like an engaged couple saving themselves for the wedding night, eagerly anticipating when they will fall naked and unashamed into each other's arms, will we be able to wait for Jesus to fully and ultimately meet our deepest needs and desires?

May these words from my friend Paige Brown, written years before she got married, be an encouragement to us:

Every problem is a theological problem, and the habitual discontent of us singles is no exception. . . .
I long to be married. My younger sister got married

two months ago. . . . Is God being any less good to
me than he is to her? The answer is a resounding NO.
God will not be less good to me because God cannot
be less good to me. It is a cosmic impossibility for God
to shortchange any of his children. . . . It is a cosmic
impossibility that anything could be better for me
right now than being single. . . . You see, we singles are
chronic amnesiacs—we forget who we are, we forget
whose we are. I am a single Christian. My identity is
not found in my marital status but in my redemptive
status. . . . I may meet someone and walk down the
aisle in the next couple of years because God is so good
to me. I may never have another date and die an old
maid at ninety-three because God is so good to me.
Not my will but his be done.[32]

Whether gay, straight, single, divorced, painfully married,
or happily married, may we find strength, resolve, and hope as
we remember that God created us ultimately for an everlasting
marriage to Jesus—a marriage that can already be ours now and
that will enjoy an intimacy even deeper than the marriage bed
in the world to come. If the biblical vision is true, then Jesus
is better than sex. His love is stronger than the strongest and
deeper than the deepest of human loves.

Chapter Nine

HOPE OR REALISM?

How is faith to endure, O God, when you allow all this scraping and tearing on us? You have allowed rivers of blood to flow, mountains of suffering to pile up, sobs to become humanity's song—all without lifting a finger that we could see. You have allowed bonds of love beyond number to be painfully snapped. If you have not abandoned us, explain yourself. We strain to hear.

—NICHOLAS WOLTERSTORFF

THE PROBLEM OF PAIN AND SUFFERING is one of the biggest reasons why people keep their distance from God. It is a problem as old as time, one that centuries of philosophy and theology have failed to resolve to our satisfaction.

If there is a God, and if this God is good and loving and in control of everything at all times, as Christians say, then why do children die? Why do marriages end in divorce? Why do people get cancer? Why are there tornadoes and hurricanes and holocausts? Why do poverty, abuse, economic inequality, racism, classism, oppression, genocide, the sex trade, and other forms of injustice continue to exist?

We are left scratching our heads. An honest look at the world causes us to resonate with Shakespeare's Macbeth more than with the idea of a loving, sovereign God—that in the end, life "is a tale told by an idiot, full of sound and fury, signifying nothing."

When suffering invades the human experience, people usually

respond in one of three ways. Some assume a "pie in the sky" perspective, clinging to superficial "Bible Band-Aids." They affirm, rightly, that "God is good all the time; all the time God is good," but they fail to acknowledge the feelings of being betrayed by God, which are expressed in the Bible as well. Pie-in-the-sky people tend to ignore honest biblical prayers such as "How long, O LORD? Will you forget me forever?"[1] and "My God, my God, why have you forsaken me?"[2] Others become cynical, maybe even dismissing the idea of God because they can't believe that a good, all-powerful God would allow horrific things to happen. Still others are hopeful realists. These are the ones who continue to believe that God is good even through suffering, and that the painful realities of life can lead to the development of perseverance, character, and hope.[3] But hopeful realists are also deeply honest about the difficult circumstances of life. While affirming that God is good all the time, they also affirm that in so many ways things are not what they are supposed to be.

The book of Job, which scholars believe is the oldest book in the Bible, wrestles with the question of suffering. God's assessment of Job is that he fears God, shuns evil, and is the most righteous person in the land. In spite of these things, Job loses all his property, all ten of his children, and his health. His first response is to fall to his knees and worship God.[4] In one of history's most stunning acts of surrender, Job says, "Naked I came from my mother's womb, and naked shall I return. The LORD gave, and the LORD has taken away; blessed be the name of the LORD."[5]

As the narrative unfolds, Job's friends do what friends do. They show up, sit with him, say nothing, and weep with him. Instead of sermons, they give him solidarity. Instead of answers, they give him themselves. But before too long, they start theorizing about Job's problem of pain and suffering. Lacking a category in which to put Job's experience, they create one for their own comfort. Wanting to defend the goodness of God, Job's friends turn into his blind critics, suggesting that this sort of suffering would not be happening to him if God weren't trying to teach him a lesson. "Confess your sins to God and forsake them," Job's friends tell him, "then God will bless you again."

Then there is Job's wife. She knows that Job is not the awful man his friends are accusing him of being. He remains the faithful man that he has always been. However, in her confusion about how a good God could allow such suffering, she snaps and turns on Job too. "Do you still hold fast to your integrity? Curse God and die."[6]

Eventually Job, too, caves in, shaking his fist at God and demanding answers. No longer able to bear the silent treatment from God, Job lashes out. "I am blameless; I regard not myself; I loathe my life. . . . Therefore I say, '[God] destroys both the blameless and the wicked.' . . . He mocks at the calamity of the innocent."[7]

The Job account presses us to ask, "Are there clear answers on this side of heaven for *why* a good God would allow suffering in his world?" Will we be satisfied with the belief held by Job's friends, that all suffering is the result of cause and effect and that we, not God, are the cause? Or will we be satisfied with the belief held by Job's wife, that the kind of God who would let good people suffer is *not* good after all, and he does *not* deserve our loyalty and affection?

Or is there some silver lining, some ray of hope to cling to even if we must cling by our fingernails? Is there a hopeful framework into which we can place legitimate grief, sorrow, and even anger about the problem of pain and suffering?

Jesus Frees Us to Be Realistic about Suffering

If Christianity has something significant to contribute to the question of suffering and evil, it is that Christianity is incredibly realistic about how messed up the world is. The Bible locates our story in an in-between time, a season of history that is sandwiched between two perfect and pain-free worlds: the Garden of Eden and the new Jerusalem.

In the beginning, God created the heavens and the earth. When he finished his work of creation, he looked at everything he had made and declared that it was *very* good. Water, earth, and sky worked in harmony together to provide a hospitable space for the plants, the animals, and our first parents, Adam and Eve. The world was perfect spiritually—man and woman were in perfect, uninterrupted communion with God every day and night.

> Christianity is incredibly realistic about how messed up the world is.

He was their God, and they were his people. Socially, man and woman were also in perfect communion with each other. There was no fighting, and there were no apologies offered, because there was nothing to fight or apologize about. In the Garden of God, Adam and Eve worked, played, ate, drank, made love, and slept deeply. They were both naked and felt no shame. Culturally, man and woman were in perfect harmony with the rest of creation. God commissioned them to name the animals and work the land—work was satisfying and meaningful. It was a true Paradise.

Then Adam and Eve, representing all of us, sought independence from God. Once they ate the forbidden fruit, everything unraveled. They ran and hid from God. They blamed each other and the serpent for what they had done. The ground was cursed and work became difficult. Relationships were also cursed, and heartache entered the picture. Pain and suffering, weakness and shame, disappointment and anticlimax have been part of the human condition ever since.

Longing for Restoration and Renewal

Paradise demonstrates not only fallen humanity's past but also a redeemed humanity's future. Just as the first chapters of the Bible describe an idyllic world, so do the last chapters. John's vision in Revelation paints the picture of a new heaven and new earth where everything broken will be restored, everything sick will be healed, everything sorrowful and sad will be turned to glory. There will no longer be any death, mourning, crying, or pain, for the old order of things will have passed away and everything will be made new.[8] The face of God will once again be accessible, his supportive presence palatable. Relationships will flourish. Work will be filled with energy and life.

If Eden and the new Jerusalem represent life as it was created to be, if *these* are the worlds we have been created for, is it any wonder that we rage against pain and suffering? Is it any wonder that we grow pessimistic and cynical and angry and sad when the world is not working the way we know it is supposed to? Our equilibrium is thrown off by suffering. It disorients us, makes us restless, and creates longing for restoration and renewal.

To rage against suffering and sorrow, therefore, is entirely natural. We were created to exist in perfection, and our hearts yearn for this. It is an agony to suffer and try to make sense of the pain.

Consider these words from C. S. Lewis after his wife, Joy, died from cancer:

> When you are happy, so happy that you have no sense of needing [God], so happy that you are tempted to feel His claims upon you as an interruption, if you remember yourself and turn to Him with gratitude and praise, you will be—or so it feels—welcomed with open arms. But go to Him when your need is desperate, when all other help is vain, and what do you find? A door slammed in your face, and a sound

of bolting and double bolting on the inside. After
that, silence.[9]

Lewis's raw honesty may come across as jarring or even blas-
phemous to some. But he is not alone in having this kind of
reaction to suffering and grief. Even David, the man after God's
own heart, reacted to suffering in a similar way. God made certain that David's reaction made it into the Psalms:

My God, my God, why have you forsaken me?
  Why are you so far from saving me, from the words
    of my groaning?
O my God, I cry by day, but you do not answer,
  and by night, but I find no rest.[10]

How long, O LORD? Will you forget me forever?
  How long will you hide your face from me?
How long must I take counsel in my soul
  and have sorrow in my heart all the day?
How long shall my enemy be exalted over me?[11]

Have you ever prayed this way? If you have, did you feel
dirty after doing so? What would you say if I told you that
this may have been one of the cleanest, purest, most Christian
prayers that you have ever prayed? What would you say if I told
you that God invites you to be honest and raw and realistic
about suffering instead of being phony about it and sweeping
it under the rug?

Consider Mary and Martha, the two sisters of Jesus' close
friend Lazarus. Jesus *loved* Lazarus. Yet Jesus allowed Lazarus to
die—and Jesus didn't even go to the funeral.

After Lazarus had been dead for four days, Jesus finally
showed up. Martha, the more intense sister, got up and got in

Jesus' face. "If you had been here, my brother would not have died."[12]

What gives, Jesus? Our brother was dying. You created galaxies by breathing. You split an ocean with a word. You made a blind man see. You walked on water. You fed thousands with a basket of bread and a handful of fish. You turned water into wine. But when we, the ones you have called your friends—when we cried out for you, when we called you in our fear and despair and helplessness and heartache . . . you kept silent. You stayed away. Why didn't you show up? Why didn't you help?

Mary did not share Martha's intensity, but she did share her concern. Instead of getting in Jesus' face, Mary kept her distance; she remained seated in the house. *What's the use in talking to Jesus about this now that our brother is dead? Perhaps Jesus isn't who we thought he was, or perhaps he is who we thought he was but he just doesn't care about us.* Only when Jesus called directly for Mary did she go out to him. Her words for Jesus were the same as her sister's: "Lord, if you had been here, my brother would not have died."[13]

Two sisters, two personalities, one conclusion:

God failed us.

The Christian Virtues of Anger and Sadness

But what if things aren't as they seem? What if God, seeming to be a million miles away, is nearer than ever? What if God, seeming to be against us, is more for us than we ever imagined?

As was the case with Job, so was the case with Mary and Martha. In both instances there was a backstory, an invisible battle in the world of God, Satan, angels, and demons, an unseen truth yet to be revealed that would have transformed the outlook of the sufferers. In the world of God there are many things we do not understand.

"The secret things belong to the LORD our God."[14]

"For now we see in a mirror dimly . . ."[15]

If we were able to know everything that God knows, if we were able to see everything that God sees, if the finite were given a glimpse of the infinite, the temporal of the eternal, our outlook on suffering and sorrow would no doubt be different. We would know with certainty that the absence of God is apparent, not real. We would see with clarity that God's plans are for our flourishing, not our ruin.

How do we know this? It's right there in the story.

The crowd of people surrounding Martha and Mary, those who *had* shown up to the funeral, began to ask among themselves the question anyone in their right mind would ask: "Could not he who opened the eyes of the blind man also have kept this man from dying?"[16]

Jesus responded in two ways. First, he preached a mini-sermon.

> Jesus said to [Martha], "I am the resurrection and the life. Whoever believes in me, though he die, yet shall he live, and everyone who lives and believes in me shall never die. Do you believe this?"[17]

What might have been going through Martha's mind? Perhaps something like this:

With all due respect, Jesus, my brother believed this. Look where it got him. Sometimes we need more than a sermon. Haven't you read the book on funeral etiquette? Haven't you studied the five stages of grief? Don't you remember Job's miserable "comforters" with their abysmal situational awareness and lack of emotional intelligence? Don't you remember Job's wife and her "sermon" that kicked Job while he was already down? We know you are God and everything, but are you so out of touch with the human condition that you don't realize that sometimes sermons add insult to injury, that they hurt more than they help?

But Jesus' curious behavior was not an indicator that he was out of touch with the human condition. It was an indicator that he was deeply *in* touch with the human condition.

Within minutes, Jesus was going to fix everything. Accessing the same divine power that he had once used to speak the universe into existence, he would speak Lazarus the dead man back to life. But before he did any of this, Jesus stopped, got angry, and wept.[18] Before he fixed a broken situation, *he entered into it and shared it.* Jesus was not pie in the sky or happy-clappy about a hard situation. He did not criticize Mary or Martha for having an ungodly or unspiritual response to their pain. Rather, by entering into their situation, he affirmed their negative reaction to suffering as *realistic*—a good, right, honest, human, *and* divine reaction to a world that wasn't functioning as it was supposed to. He entered in. He shared and felt their sorrows before mending their sorrows. He does the same for us.

> He was . . . a man of sorrows, and acquainted with grief. . . . Surely he has borne our griefs and carried our sorrows. . . . He was crushed . . . and with his wounds we are healed . . . although he had done no violence, and there was no deceit in his mouth. Yet it was the will of the LORD to crush him; he has put him to grief. . . . Out of the anguish of his soul he shall see and be satisfied. . . . He poured out his soul to death . . . and makes intercession for the transgressors.[19]

When Jesus saw that Mary and the Jews who were with her were weeping, Jesus was "deeply moved in his spirit and greatly troubled." When Jesus came to the tomb of Lazarus, again he was "deeply moved."[20] Here, the English translation does not do justice to the original Greek, which says that Jesus was *indignant.* Angry. Fuming. Furious like a hornet about to sting, a bull about to attack, or a lion about to kill.

Jesus was not angry *at* Martha or Mary or the mourners who questioned him. On the contrary, he was angry *for* them. He was angry against the bully who had hurt them, against the unwelcome invader who had assaulted their peace and torn apart their family, against the brute who had smacked them around and made them cry. Jesus was angry at death.

Sometimes I wonder about people who don't believe in a God who gets angry. "My God is a God of love, not anger," some say. But don't we get angry when the people we love are bullied? Do we really want a God who doesn't get angry at death, the biggest bully of all?

> Jesus saw death. Jesus saw tears. And Jesus was furious about it.

Recently I saw a pamphlet on the Internet that an elementary school created for its students. The pamphlet was written for students who are bullied by other students. The pamphlet says that if students are bullied, they should do the following: refuse to get mad, treat the person who is being mean as if he or she is trying to help you, do not be afraid, do not verbally defend yourself, and do not attack. If someone physically hurts you, do not get angry; do not tell on bullies, do not be a sore loser, and learn to laugh at yourself.

Thank God this isn't the pamphlet he gave us as an instruction manual for dealing with oppression and injustice and bullying and suffering and sorrow and death.

Instead, when suffering and death come in as invaders, Jesus gets realistic, and Jesus gets mad. He turns over tables in the Temple and flares his nostrils like a bull about to go into battle. He assumes a fighting posture with every intention of eliminating the bully of death.

Jesus saw death. Jesus saw tears. And Jesus was furious about it.

Jesus also got sad, especially when he encountered the soft-spoken Mary. As Mary and the others led him to Lazarus's tomb, his anger was joined by sadness.

Jesus personally responds to our fuming and sadness. Feisty Martha got to see Jesus get angry at death. Tenderhearted Mary got to see him cry. Two unique women witnessed two unique responses from their Lord and Friend. Jesus, who is the fullness of the image of God, not only sympathized with them, he did so *according to their uniqueness*. Jesus arched his back toward the bully for Martha's sake. Then he shed tears for Mary's sake. Perhaps Nicholas Wolterstorff was thinking of Jesus' tears when he wrote this reflection in response to the premature death of his son:

> We strain to hear [God in our sorrows]. But instead
> of hearing an answer we catch the sight of God himself
> scraped and torn. Through our tears we see the tears
> of God. . . . Perhaps his sorrow is splendor.[21]

Jesus is the resurrection and the life. The ones who believe in him, though they die, yet shall they live.[22] He will call them forth from their graves just as he called Lazarus from the grave mere minutes after getting angry and crying about Lazarus's death.

Jesus wants to fix everything that's broken about us and everything that's broken around us. But before he does this, he wants us to know that he is with us and for us *in* what's broken about us and around us. He shares our situation. He is a warrior and a champion against the bully, but also much more. He is a friend who sticks closer than a brother, a mother hen who gathers her fragile chicks under her wings, and an advocate who shares our grief and our tears—especially, and ironically, during the times when he seems most distant. He is a sympathetic realist.

Jesus, the sympathetic realist, reminds us that everything is broken.

At least it is for now.

Jesus Gives Us Hope for the Future

Suffering is not the end of the story for those whose hope is anchored in Jesus. Flannery O'Connor wrote that things like virgin birth and incarnation and resurrection and a pain-free life are the "true laws" and that death, decay, and destruction, rather than being ultimate reality, are a temporary suspension of these laws.[23] The life we are living now, the one characterized by groaning and decay and death and mourning and crying and pain, is the in-between chapter of a Story that both begins and ends in Paradise. Because of sin, these things have come into play; because the wages of sin is death, when we eat forbidden fruit, whatever its form, we will surely die.[24] But God, being rich in mercy and not desiring that we should perish, has pledged to clean up the mess we have made for ourselves and make all things new.

Jesus said to [Martha], "Your brother will rise again. . . . I am the resurrection and the life. Whoever believes in me, though he die, yet shall he live, and everyone who lives and believes in me shall never die. Do you believe this?"[25]

Then I saw a new heaven and a new earth, for the first heaven and the first earth had passed away, and the sea was no more. And I saw the holy city, new Jerusalem, coming down out of heaven from God, prepared as a bride adorned for her husband. And I heard a loud voice from the throne saying, "Behold, the dwelling place of God is with man. He will dwell with them, and they will be his people, and God himself will be with them as their God. He will wipe away every tear from their eyes, and death shall be no more, neither shall there be mourning, nor crying, nor pain anymore, for the former things have passed away." And he who was seated on the throne said, "Behold, I am making all things new. . . . Write this down, for these words are trustworthy and true."[26]

I once heard N. T. Wright say that hope is imagining God's future into the present. Tim Keller says similar things when he invokes the words of Tolkien's Samwise Gamgee, who speculates that one day everything sad will come untrue, and C. S. Lewis, who talks about how heaven will work backward and turn even agony into glory.[27]

What these men are saying is the same thing that Jesus was saying to Martha and that John, the beloved disciple, envisioned when he saw a glimpse of the new Jerusalem. In the future world, those who suffered in this life but who anchored their hope in the next will look back on death, mourning, crying, and pain as if they were part of a nightmare, a suspension of reality versus reality itself. Everything sad will come untrue. Their capacity to enjoy life will be even greater than it would be had they never lived through a nightmare in the first place.

Once when I was six years old, my parents were away on vacation. On the night of their return, the babysitter woke me up to tell me that she had some bad news. An airplane had crashed and there were no survivors—and it *might* have been the flight my parents were on.

Dear babysitters,
    Don't deliver life-altering bad news to a six-year-old

child unless you have first confirmed that said bad news is true.

Yours truly,

Every six-year-old child

Ours was not a Christian home, but that night I prayed to God. It was basic instinct. *God, if you're up there, please bring my parents back. Make them not be dead. Make them not be dead. Make them not be dead.*

Two hours later my parents walked through the door.

I have never loved and enjoyed my parents more than I did for the rest of that evening.

Have you ever awakened from a nightmare and been flooded with relief that what you dreamed about was not true? It's the same feeling people get when the doctor says the cancer is gone or the police call with the news that a lost child has been found. Not only are you relieved that the terrible conditions in which you lived are gone, you also enjoy and celebrate and delight in what has been returned to you more than you ever had before.

This is what God promises to those who anchor their hope in Jesus, who is the resurrection and the life. *Though we die, yet shall we live.* Reality will be rescued once and for all from the nightmares. No longer will there be the need to *imagine* God's future into the present, because God's future will *be* in the present. Now we see him as through a dim mirror. Then we will see him face to face.[28]

If we knew everything that God knows, if we saw everything that God sees . . .

Martha and Mary had a small glimpse of God's future just a few moments after Jesus got angry and cried about death. Jesus prayed to his Father in heaven and then shouted into the tomb of his friend, "Lazarus, come out!" And the dead man came out.[29]

A Reason to Fight against Suffering

I sometimes wonder why Jesus decided to raise Lazarus from the dead. On the one hand, it made for an unexpected and welcome celebration for Lazarus, his sisters, and the community. It was yet another demonstration that Jesus is stronger than nature, even stronger than death. But Lazarus was going to die again. Eventually there would be another funeral. Why subject everyone to another season of grief?

While we are on the subject, why do we fight against suffering and injustice and evil at all? Is there any point in fighting disease and cancer when the mortality rate for human beings is always going to be one death per one person? Is there any point in fighting poverty when even Jesus said that no matter what we do, the poor are always going to be with us? Is there any point in fighting to recover a broken marriage or friendship when it would be easier, and it would feel much less painful and costly, just to cut our losses and move on?

> Jesus has already begun his renovation project of making all things new.

Why did Jesus bring Lazarus back? Because Jesus came to bring God's Kingdom to earth as it is in heaven, not only to imagine God's future into the present but to bring glimpses and foretastes of God's future into the present. In a world in which God's reality is suspended for a time, Jesus zealously refuses to allow death, mourning, crying, and pain to dictate the story line. Perhaps this is why Jesus taught more about the Kingdom of God than about any other subject.

Jesus invites us to share his perspective—to believe that invisible realities are even truer than the visible ones. He wants us to know and remember that life conquers death and that he has already begun his renovation project of making all things new. This is why Jesus says that we, too, must wage war against conditions that threaten the flourishing of the people and world that God has made. In teaching us to pray, "Your kingdom come, your will be done on earth as it is in heaven," Jesus invites us to join him in this fight, to boldly shout "Come out!" into tombs, because, as C. S. Lewis reminds us, Christianity is a fighting religion:

> Confronted with a cancer or a slum the Pantheist can say, "If you could only see it from the divine point of view, you would realise that this also is God." The Christian replies, "Don't talk damned nonsense." For Christianity is a fighting religion. It thinks God made the world—that space and time, heat and cold, and all the colours and tastes, and all the animals and vegetables, are things that God "made up out of His head" as a man makes up a story. But it also thinks that a great many things have gone wrong with the world that God made and that God insists, and insists very loudly, on our putting them right again.[30]

A Reason to Remain Hopeful

Sometimes the cancer is not cured. Sometimes the slum remains a slum. Sometimes the marriage fails and the friendship ends. Sometimes our hearts break. We suffer; we hurt; we experience loss; we ache. In the midst of these very real battles, Jesus speaks to us out of his own sorrow and grief to remind us that, in the end, hope will win. In the end, life will overcome death, joy will overcome sorrow, freedom will overcome bondage, and triumph will overcome loss.

Still, we wait.

When Jesus said, "I am the resurrection and the life," it wasn't just a prediction about the future. It was also an identity statement. Whenever Jesus uses the words *I am* to describe himself, he is claiming to be God. *I am* is Old Testament language that Jews like Mary and Martha understood to mean one thing. They would instantly remember Moses and the burning bush, out of which the Maker of the universe spoke the words, "Say this to the people of Israel, 'I AM has sent me to you.'"[31]

The same God who created the galaxies with a breath, who split the ocean with words, and who calls a dead man out of a tomb is the God who is going to make all things new and whose words are trustworthy and true.

Yet we struggle to lay hold of these realities in a broken here and now.

During occasional seasons in my adult life I have suffered from insomnia, anxiety, and panic attacks. Whenever these seasons have come, the anxiety was triggered by fear about the future. The triggers for me fall into three categories or questions. First, am I going to be alone? Second, am I going to get an incurable disease? Third, am I going to be able to provide for the people who depend on me?

Part of the way that I have confronted the anxiety has been to work with a professional counselor. Several years ago, during a particularly anxious season, my counselor observed how prone I was to meditate on worst-case scenarios. Instead of coming up with all the reasons why my fears were irrational and would probably never come to be, she challenged me to assume that my fears were true and face them head-on. She challenged me to think about, and then speak out loud, what the *long-term*, worst-case scenario would be if I ended up alone, or sick, or could not provide for my loved ones. "Let's just imagine for a minute that each and every one of your fears was real and actual. Then, let's fast-forward a hundred years into the future. Where is the worst-case scenario going to take you, Scott? You preach the answer to this question to others all the time. Let's pause for a moment and see if you can preach it to yourself."

If I end up alone, the worst-case scenario is that Jesus is the resurrection and the life, and those who believe in him, though they die, yet shall they live. God has set a place for me at the wedding feast of Jesus, and I will be part of the church, his bride, forever. He puts the lonely into an eternal family. He will never leave or forsake me. The long-term, worst-case scenario is that I will never be alone, that I will always be known, loved, and received.

If I get a disease, the worst-case scenario is that Jesus is the resurrection and the life, and those who believe in him, though they die, yet shall they live. Just as Jesus' body has been raised incorruptible and will no longer be subject to decay, so will mine be. He forgives all my sins and will heal all my diseases and crown me with love and compassion and redeem my life from every pit. The long-term, worst-case scenario is that I will be happy, healthy, strong, and whole forevermore.

If I cannot provide, the worst-case scenario is that Jesus is the resurrection and the life, and those who believe in him, though they die, yet shall they live. Jesus is rich. Everything in heaven and earth is his, and every square inch and every penny, nickel, dime, and dollar belong to him. But Jesus is more than rich; he is the true riches. Whether I live in poverty or wealth, I will always be able to say with the Puritan who was stripped to nothing but a piece of bread and a glass of water, "What? All of this and Jesus Christ, too?" The long-term, worst-case scenario is that I will inherit a wealth that will never spoil, perish, or fade—the wealth being Jesus himself. This inheritance will be not only for me but also for those depending on me who have anchored their own futures in *his* provision, not mine.

Is it any wonder that the most repeated command in the Bible is "Do not fear"?

God's long-term promises are infinitely more real than any present, broken reality. It takes a God-given faith for us to see these things and let ourselves be impacted by them emotionally, spiritually, relationally, and otherwise. But with this God-given faith, we who are realistic about suffering can also live in hope because the broken reality in which we live is not the ultimate reality. Suffering, sorrow, and death will not be a part of life. All nightmares, imagined and real, will come to an end. Everything sad will come untrue. These words are trustworthy and true.

Christ has died. Christ is risen. Christ will come again.

Thanks be to God.

Chapter Ten

SELF-ESTEEM OR GOD-ESTEEM?

*When I get honest, I admit I am a bundle of paradoxes. I believe and
I doubt, I hope and get discouraged, I love and I hate, I feel bad about
feeling good, I feel guilty about not feeling guilty. I am trusting and
suspicious. I am honest and I still play games. Aristotle said I am a rational
animal; I say I am an angel with an incredible capacity for beer.*

—BRENNAN MANNING

THE GREEK MYTH OF NARCISSUS CAN HAUNT ME. Though
the story is historically untrue, from a personal point of view it
could not be *more* true.

As the story goes, Narcissus is a young man widely known for
his beauty. One day while walking in the woods, a nymph named
Echo notices him. Struck by his beauty, she swiftly falls in love
with him and begins following him. Eventually, the enamored
Echo discloses her feelings to Narcissus, who swiftly rejects her.
Crestfallen, she retreats and spends the rest of her life in sad isolation. Eventually nothing is left of her but a faint echo. Nemesis,
the goddess of revenge, is sympathetic to the adoring Echo and
therefore enraged at Narcissus. She lures him to a pool where she
draws his attention to his own reflection in the water. Thinking it
another creature, Narcissus falls in love with the image of himself.
Once he discovers he will never be able to draw closer to the face
in the pool, Narcissus dies from unfulfilled self-love.

For those who prefer a more lighthearted making of the point, there's also the all-too-relatable movie line from Groucho Marx. After going on and on about himself to a young lady, he stops and says, "That's enough about me. Let's talk about you. What do *you* think about me?"

Nobody likes to be around a self-absorbed person, whether mythological or real. But we must admit that in many ways we *are* this person. Craving affirmation, we spend large amounts of time gazing at our own image—investing extraordinary amounts of time, resources, and energy to control what others think about us. We draw attention to the good and censor out the bad that we find in ourselves. We calculate. We strategize. We self-promote. We shield ourselves from criticism. We save face. We seek the upper hand. We want to ensure that we are perceived as *winners*. Isn't this why we so swiftly choose sides on any number of issues, including the ones featured in this book?

I was the fastest boy in my fifth-grade class. Because of this I was given the honor of representing my class against other fifth-grade boys on "field day" in the fifty-yard dash. I remember how driven I was to win the event. I ran time trials in my backyard, ate a lot of spaghetti, and got plenty of rest in anticipation of sweet victory. I was new to the school, and the fifty-yard dash was my chance to earn the admiration of my new classmates. There was also a girl named Holly—so beautiful that the mere sight of her caused the song "Dream Weaver" to play in my head. If only I could distinguish myself as the fastest boy in the *entire* fifth grade, Holly would certainly be mine.

What I did not know at the time was that another boy, Doug, would also compete in the fifty-yard dash, and he was just as fast—*exactly* as fast—as I was. To make a long story short, Doug and I tied for first place. The initial field of ten runners was reduced to just the two of us. To identify a clear winner (there was only one first-place ribbon), the teachers made Doug and me run a second heat, then a third, then a fourth against only each other. In each of the four heats, we both crossed the finish line at exactly the same time. The school buses would soon arrive, so the teachers crowned Doug and me co-victors in the fifty-yard dash. (I have no idea what they did with that lone first-place ribbon; I must have blocked it out of my memory.)

From that point forward I saw Doug not as a fellow champion but as a rival, an archnemesis if you will. We had unfinished business. To make matters worse, Holly paid no attention to me. She chose instead to set her affections on Billy, the stand-alone winner of the fifth-grade long jump. It was a harsh lesson to learn—nobody wants to hold hands with someone who *tied* for first place.

After fifth grade, Doug and I went our separate ways and on to different middle schools. We would never see each other again. Or, more truthfully, *he* would never see *me* again.

About a decade after Doug and I tied for first place, the Olympics were on television. I was in the kitchen preparing dinner when the national anthem began to play, so I went into the living room to celebrate the latest American gold medalist. There I stood as the music played. Staring at me through the television was a tall, confident, perfectly chiseled, take-no-prisoners specimen of a man. It was Doug.

Disturbingly unable to celebrate Doug's victory, I moped my way back to the kitchen. As I stood over the macaroni and cheese, I swiftly blocked what I had just seen out of my memory.

But that wasn't the end of the story. Eight years later, while watching the Olympics again, but this time with my wife, Patti, the broadcasters decided to televise a throwback of Doug's award ceremony. As we watched, I did two things: first, I said to Patti, "How cool is that? Did I ever tell you that that guy and I tied for first place in a fifth-grade race?" As I boasted this news to Patti, I also said to my own soul, *A gold medal? Big deal. I have a master's degree.*

As much as I hate to admit it, the Greek myth of Narcissus is no myth to me. It is my reality. Is it yours? Enough about me. Let's talk about you. What do *you* think about me?

Pride As Rivalry

In his magnificent work *Mere Christianity*, C. S. Lewis says this about pride:

> There is one vice of which no man in the world is free; which every one in the world loathes when he sees it in someone else. . . . The vice I am talking of is Pride or Self-Conceit. . . . It was through Pride that the devil became the devil: Pride leads to every other vice: it is the complete anti-God state of mind. . . .
>
> Now what you want to get clear is that Pride is *essentially* competitive—is competitive by its very nature—while the other vices are competitive only, so to speak, by accident. Pride gets no pleasure out of having something, only out of having more of it than the next man. We say that people are proud of being rich, or clever, or good-looking, but they are not. They are proud of being richer, or cleverer, or better-looking than others. . . . It is the comparison that makes you proud: the pleasure of being above the rest.[1]

Lewis taps into the psychology of why I reacted the way I did to Doug's gold medal. He reminds us why we crave recognition and so desperately want to be *the* best instead of simply being *our* best, and why we don't want to share our glory with another. Pride, Lewis says, is essentially competitive. We *have* to pick a side and fight our battle in order to convince God, others, and even ourselves that we are significant, valuable, and worthy of being noticed. That's why so often, our disagreements get ugly. Once we've chosen a side, we can't acknowledge anything good about the other side. We have to *win outright*.

The Pharisee prays, "God, I thank you that I am not like other men, extortioners, unjust, adulterers, or even like this tax collector. I fast twice a week; I give tithes of all that I get."[2] Interestingly, the original Greek says that the man literally prays these things *to his own soul*. He is not giving credit or thanks to God for transforming him into a man of virtue. Rather, he is expressing his emotional neediness through, of all things, a self-exalting "prayer." He is trying to convince himself that he is superior to the nearest man standing by. By belittling others and rehearsing his own achievements, he is trying to build up his self-esteem. By creating a blown-up caricature of himself (*I am so superior*) and a diminished caricature of the tax collector and other "sinners" (*they are so inferior*), by choosing to side with himself and against other "lesser people," he is trying to medicate his own wounded ego. He portrays himself as large and in charge and belittles others to compensate for how small he is in his own eyes.

> We crave recognition; we desperately want to be *the* best instead of simply being *our* best.

We create caricatures for the very same reasons. To caricature is to exaggerate the less flattering features of other people as the Pharisee does. She didn't merely disclose a secret about her friend in a moment of temptation. She is a *gossip*. He didn't just lose self-control and eat a fifth slice of pizza. He is a *glutton*. She isn't merely conservative in her politics. She is a *right-wing* conservative (or a *socialist* liberal, as the case may be). She isn't merely a bad driver. She is a *woman driver*. He didn't just forget our anniversary. He is a *terrible husband*.

"God, thank you that I am not like *him*. . . ."

"God, thank you that I am not like *her*. . . ."

"God, thank you that I am not like *them*. . . ."

Yuck. And yet, truth be told, we identify. Especially when we're afraid or feeling threatened, we start to divide the world between "us" and "them," between those who matter and those who don't, between those who are competent and those who struggle, between those who are enlightened and those who aren't, between the good people and the bad people. We are essentially competitive by nature. This explains our posture. This explains why it feels so natural for us to take sides in destructive ways on all sorts of subjects—politics, the use of money, parenting, sexuality, philosophy, theology, and even our favorite (and least favorite) "brands" of Christianity.

Pride As Self-Loathing

Where does this rivalry come from? What is its origin? Why, as Yale theologian Miroslav Volf so aptly says it, do we instinctively "exclude the enemy from the community of humans even as [we] exclude [ourselves] from the community of sinners"?[3] Interestingly, the Bible tells us that the root cause of pride and an unhealthy rivalry spirit is not self-love but self-loathing.

In Philippians 2:3, Paul warns of two toxic ingredients that make up the deadly sin of pride. These two ingredients are *selfish ambition* and *vain conceit*.

Selfish Ambition

Selfish ambition makes us see virtually every situation and interaction as a competition. Selfish ambition leads us into the habit of comparing ourselves to others. We have to see ourselves not only as rich, but *more* rich. Not just clever, but *more* clever. Not merely good looking, but *better* looking.

For example, think about how we react to the circumstances in other people's lives. When I saw the Olympic gold hanging from the neck of my fifth-grade rival, my first impulse was to protect my own ego. More than *ten* years later, I somehow still needed to feel that he had not surpassed me. *I'll see your Olympic medal and raise you a master's degree.* When selfish ambition resides in us, we become threatened by the good fortune of others. Their blessings become our curses. Why does *he* get the girl while I remain alone? Why does *she* get the promotion while I am stuck in this less significant, lower-paying role? Why was *he* elected when my candidate is clearly superior? Why was *she* given such good looks while I remain dissatisfied every time I look in the mirror?

Even worse, selfish ambition can ignite in us a secret enjoyment of the misfortune and failures of others. An NFL running back is accused of murdering his wife, and the world wants access to every detail of the case—and gets it. A teenage celebrity checks in to an addiction recovery center for the third time, and the world cries, "Shame on her." A well-known pastor is caught in a sex and drug scandal and becomes a talk-show punch line for months on end. A famous actress struggles mightily with an eating addiction and with being one hundred pounds overweight. She is asked to be on a reality TV show, the star of which will be her body weight.

Every time a well-known person is hurting or falls from grace, the news outlets, social media, and blogosphere immediately light up. We seem to thrive on the public failure, shame, and misfortune of others. We are "concerned," "saddened," "appalled," "enraged," "beside ourselves" . . . and so very glad to talk about it. But why? Why is there such an appetite for the downfall and belittling of others? Why is the misfortune of others such a hot topic for us? Welcome to the fallen human condition.

Selfish ambition can be ugly. It can also be so sad. I will never forget the sinking feeling I had after reading in the *New York Daily News* about Kelly Osbourne, the daughter of rock-and-roll star Ozzy Osbourne and his wife, Sharon. After disappearing from the public eye for a long stretch of time, Kelly reemerged during New York City's 2010 Fashion Week. Suddenly she had a newfound confidence after losing forty-two pounds. The once famously morose, chubby reality TV star now had a new curvy body, and along with it, a new aura of poise. The world, for a moment, took notice. When asked about why she lost the weight, she replied, "I took more hell for being fat than I did for being an absolute raging drug addict. . . . I'm really proud to look in the mirror and not hate every single thing I see. I no longer think, 'Why don't you look like this girl or that girl?'"[4]

We should applaud Kelly Osbourne for such an accomplishment. Losing forty-two pounds and overcoming drug addiction is no small feat. It takes massive amounts of resolve, self-control, and discipline. That being said, it should also sadden us how the shame narrative of our culture played such a hand in her accomplishments.

Said the culture: *You are a loser if you are fat—worse than a raging drug addict, even.*

Said Osbourne to her own soul: *Why don't you look like this girl or that girl?*

This shows that the need to compare ourselves with others does not always come from a place of bravado and arrogance. Sometimes it comes from a frightened, lonely, shame-filled place where the only instinct is survival—like a minnow swimming among sharks.

Vain Conceit

The second impulse Paul warns against is what he calls *vain conceit.*[5] The Greek term literally means "empty glory" or "glory hunger." Vain conceit is the driver behind our craving for attention and approval—our insatiable appetite to be recognized, appreciated, praised, and adored by other people.

This particular impulse starts from a good place. The beginning chapters of Genesis tell us that we are made in the image of God, whose essence and nature demand that he be made much of. It is not surprising that we as image bearers desire the same thing.

Patti and I have seen this in our daughters' quests for attention. In their younger years, Abby's and Ellie's constant refrain was, "Mom, Dad, WATCH ME!" It didn't matter what they were doing; they simply wanted to do it with an audience. Watch me swing. Watch me hang on the monkey bars. Watch me jump on the trampoline. Watch me ride the tricycle. Once, one of our daughters asked me to watch her while she read a book . . . silently to herself! As they grow older, the watch-worthy items become more sophisticated: How does my hair look? Do you like this dress and does it go with these shoes? Did you see my report card? Are you proud of me? And it's not only children who feel this way. Patti has to remind me on occasion that her preferred love language is the language of affirming words. I'm pretty certain it's mine as well. Regardless of whether it is your love language, this desire is in us all, and we never outgrow it. We want to be praised and noticed. In its purest form, this is good and even godlike.

But things go south when an appropriate desire for praise morphs into a misplaced hunger for approval. This vain conceit,

> If we lose the applause, we feel worthless.

or insatiable approval-hunger, can lead us to depend deeply or even exclusively on the attention and applause of others. If we lose the applause, we feel worthless.

Consider the great tennis champion Chris Evert. For many years as the top-ranked women's tennis player in the world, Evert accumulated a staggering eighteen grand-slam titles. She was accustomed to being on top of the comparison pyramid. Everyone in women's tennis wanted to be *her*. And why not? All those victories, all that attention, all that money, and there was also the slim, athletic, unattainable body . . .

Yet, as is true for so many professional athletes who peak in their twenties, Evert experienced an identity crisis when her ability to win matches was overcome by the aging process. In a 1990 interview with *Good Housekeeping*, she shared these words about her inner world after retiring from tennis:

> I had no idea who I was, or what I could be away from tennis. I was depressed and afraid because so much of my life had been defined by my being a tennis champion. I was completely lost. Winning made me feel like I was somebody. It made me feel pretty. It was like being hooked on a drug. I needed the wins, the applause, in order to have an identity.[6]

I must say that such transparency about one's inner struggles—especially from a legend such as Chris Evert—is very endearing to me. Her courage to go public with her inner struggles, even more than her many tennis victories, makes her a champion in my eyes. Her courage to confess her frailty helps the rest of us face our sense of loss and feelings of smallness. Personally, it gives *me* hope that I am not alone in the world with my embarrassing *I have a master's degree* reactions to the adult success of my fifth-grade, field-day rival.

Why do we feel insignificant? Why do we feel we have to compete? Why do we have to take sides? Why, like the Pharisee who prays pathetic prayers to his own soul, do we try to bolster our own sense of righteousness by treating others with contempt? Because winning makes us feel like we are somebody. Winning makes us feel pretty. We think that we need the wins, the applause, in order to have an identity.

But there's good news for us. It doesn't have to be this way.

Humility As the Answer to Rivalries and Narcissism

It is quite possible for approval junkies to begin putting selfish ambition and vain conceit to rest. It is possible for us as incomplete, frail, fallen human beings to have high levels of confidence and poise. But first we must reject the popular assumption that true self-esteem depends upon bravado and the sort of hollow self-talk once popularized by the Stuart Smalley character on *Saturday Night Live*: "I'm good enough, I'm smart enough, and doggone it, people like me."

Consider these words about self-esteem from the *Harvard Business Review*:

> If you look under the *Self-Help* heading on Amazon, you'll find roughly 5,000 books listed under the subhead *Self-Esteem*. The vast majority of these books aim to not only tell you why your self-esteem might be low, but to show you how to get your hands on some more of it. It's a thriving business because self-esteem is, at least in Western cultures, considered the bedrock of individual success. You can't possibly get ahead in life, the logic goes, unless you believe you are perfectly awesome.
>
> And of course you must *be* perfectly awesome in order to keep believing that you are—so you live in

quiet terror of making mistakes, and feel devastated when you do. Your only defense is to refocus your attention on all the things you do well, mentally stroking your own ego until it has forgotten this horrible episode of unawesomeness and moved on to something more satisfying.

When you think about it, this doesn't exactly sound like a recipe for success, does it? Indeed, recent reviews of the research on high self-esteem have come to the troubling conclusion that it's not all it's cracked up to be. High self-esteem does not predict better performance or greater success. And though people with high self-esteem do think they're more successful, objectively, they are not. High self-esteem does not make you a more effective leader, a more appealing lover, more likely to lead a healthy lifestyle, or more attractive and compelling in an interview. But if Stuart Smalley is wrong, and high self-esteem (along with daily affirmations of your own terrificness) is not the answer to all your problems, then what is?[7]

The Bible's answer to the "problem of self-esteem" is the virtue of humility. According to the Bible, two things are true. First, we are sinners in the sight of God. We fall woefully short of being the people that he created us to be. We are not perfect, and we fail to abide by even our own standards. Second, in Christ and because of Christ we are not only forgiven but have received an irrevocable mark of *favor*. We are God's adopted daughters and sons, fearfully and wonderfully made, the apples of his eye, who cannot be separated from his love or snatched out of his hand. Through Christ we are *highly esteemed* by our Judge and Maker, who also calls himself our Father.[8]

Why should we frantically try to bolster our own self-esteem when we are esteemed in this way by the one who spoke galaxies into being? Why should we choose sides against others in order to feel better about ourselves? Why should we diminish "them" with negative caricatures to make us feel a little less ashamed of what we see in the mirror? Christ has taken care of all of this. We no longer have to position ourselves against the other side. We no longer have to pray pathetic prayers to our own souls.

Humility Defined

Maybe you've heard this definition of humility: "True humility is not thinking less of yourself; it is thinking of yourself less." Humility is a virtue we admire in others and desire most in our family members, closest friends, and confidants. Unlike pompous people, the humble are a breath of fresh air. Unlike approval junkies, the humble are low maintenance and approachable. Though not perfect, they are generally kind, modest, agreeable, respectful, and deferential in nature. They treat others as being *more* significant than themselves.[9]

Best of all, you never sense that humble people want to be your rivals. They aren't the type to put you in your place. Even when they disagree with you, you sense that they are in your corner. They respect your dignity. They will not disparage your dignity or reputation, nor will they take sides with you in disparaging somebody else. They don't need to, because ironically, humble people are also among the most confident. They possess a solid inner core and are among the most secure, emotionally healthy people in the world. They make you want to be a better human being. By their mere presence they call you to higher ground . . . to be and become the very best version of yourself, the person that God has created you to be.

It's no wonder that we all want humble people as our friends. But how do *we* become the kind of people that we ourselves desire as friends?

Hope As the Fruit of Humility

Humility begins with the courage of Chris Evert. It begins by admitting that we are emotionally needy and have leaned on dysfunctional, disordered loves to fill that need. We are weary of staring at our own reflection in the pool. We are weary of having to depend on winning, conquering, and caricaturing others in order to "feel pretty."

This kind of admission is the gateway to joy and confidence. It is the gateway to true humility and a genuine, healthy self-esteem. It is the gateway not to thinking less of ourselves, but to thinking of ourselves less, so as to make space for love and kindness toward our fellow human beings who bear the image of God.

The late Jack Miller is often quoted as saying, "Cheer up! You're a worse sinner than you ever dared imagine, and you're more loved than you ever dared hope."

Why is this good news? Why is knowing that we are "worse sinners than we ever dared imagine" a reason to "cheer up"? My sincere hope is that the next two sentences will represent a turning point in your thinking, if they have not already. There is no condemnation for those who are in Christ Jesus. Furthermore, there is nothing in all creation that is able to separate you from the love of God, which is in Christ Jesus.[10]

Translation: Jesus Christ lived the perfect life that *we* should have lived—but we did not because we could not. And he died the sinner's death that *we* should have died—but we will never have to because he did so for us. Because Jesus died the sinner's death in our place, God has no punitive anger left for us—only love, compassion, and a plan to transform us into the likeness of Jesus. Because Jesus lived the perfect life in our place, we are covered with what the Bible calls the robe of Jesus' righteousness. In the sight of God, it is *as if*—and it will forever be *as if*—the perfect validating record of Jesus Christ was accomplished by us. Through Jesus, we are credited with his perfection and beauty. Through Jesus we are highly esteemed.

What does this mean for those who place their trust in Jesus Christ? It means paradox. It means we have been brought into something that no other religion, philosophy, or worldview can offer: a full welcome into the family of God, whereby we are fully known *and* fully loved, completely exposed *and* not rejected, temporally broken *and* everlastingly significant, small in comparison to the Creation *and* magnificent in the Creator's eyes.

God does not simply bear with you, put up with you, or tolerate you. He actually likes you. He enjoys you. He is proud of you. He esteems you highly.

> In the sight of God, it is *as if*—and it will forever be *as if*—the perfect validating record of Jesus Christ was accomplished by us.

Why We Mustn't Skip the Genealogies

The most overlooked sections of the Christmas accounts in the Bible are the genealogies of Jesus' ancestry.[11] I am especially moved by the bluntness of the genealogies in terms of whose names were included in them, because in those days a person's genealogy worked like a résumé. Your ancestry was your validating record. It gave you your credentials. Just as we feature our best accomplishments and omit our worst failures from a résumé, the ancients would feature ancestors they held in highest esteem, and omit those of whom they were ashamed. Herod the Great, for example, destroyed his genealogy so he wouldn't be judged on the basis of his ancestry.

Who made it onto Jesus' "résumé"? Whom did the Spirit inspire the Gospel writers to include on Jesus' family tree? Several types of people.

First, there are those we would expect—people who were great in the world's eyes. Of course David and Solomon were included. Who wouldn't want the world to know that they came from the lineage of two famous, beloved kings? Also on the list is Abraham, who was so wealthy he could have been on the cover of *Forbes*.

Why am I encouraged by these heavy hitters on Jesus' esteemed list? For several reasons, not the least of which is because of what Chris Evert's instincts told her: age eventually displaces awesomeness. Eventually, death will bring all finite human greatness to an abrupt end. Remember why these people are on Jesus' list in the first place . . . they are *ancestors*. They. Are. Dead. People.

Yikes. Yet these genealogies remind us that Jesus, the everlasting King, has the power and resolve to give us a name that will outlast death. As Job confidently said, "I know that my Redeemer lives, and at the last he will stand upon the earth. And after my skin has been thus destroyed, yet in my flesh I shall see God."[12]

But then Jesus throws us for a loop. Who else is on his résumé? Also included are men and women whom the world did not notice at all. Before David became king, he had been small in the world's eyes, considered by his father to be an insignificant and forgettable son—the "runt" who worked out in the fields with sheep. Joseph and Mary were two unassuming teenagers from the small town of Nazareth, so poor that they could afford to give only the poor man's offering of a turtledove at the Temple. And then there is Cosam. We know nothing about Cosam because he is not mentioned anywhere else in Scripture or history. But as the late Francis Schaeffer would say, in the eyes of God "there are no little people."

Finally, Jesus' résumé includes people who led messy lives, who made mistakes, who lived with oceans of regret. David, as Matthew 1:6 reminds us, was "the father of Solomon *by the wife of Uriah*" (emphasis added). This conjures up memories of a low point in Israel's history, when a beloved king committed adultery with the wife of one of his most loyal soldiers, then arranged for the soldier to be murdered to keep the story from going public. Yet God esteems David enough to include him in Jesus' genealogy. Abraham, who exposed his wife in order to protect his own hide, is on the list as well. There is Jacob, whose name means "deceiver." (Can you imagine how difficult it must have been for Jacob to meet girls? "Well, hello there. What's your name? My name is Liar.") Rahab, a foreigner and a prostitute, is on the list. Tamar, who disguised herself as a prostitute to trick her father-in-law into sleeping with her, is on the list. Adam made it onto Jesus' list as well. Adam, the one who brought sin into the world and ruined things for the human race.

If There's Hope for Them, There's Hope for Us

If there is hope for these people, if Jesus openly values and claims them, then surely there is hope for us, yes? Yes, indeed. Jesus Christ is the answer and cure to Narcissus's obsession with himself, Kelly Osbourne's professed self-hatred, Chris Evert's professed decline in self-worth, and Scott Sauls's inability to celebrate Doug's Olympic gold medal ten years after the field-day episode. Jesus is the answer to whatever burdens you, as well.

To be esteemed by Jesus is to be free. It allows us to be honest with the world and ourselves. We are not what we are supposed to be. We are incomplete works in progress—shattered, wrecked, ruined, weak, wounded, sick, and sore. And yet . . . and yet. We have a resource at our disposal that ensures that we, through Jesus Christ, are significant in the eyes of the only Judge who matters. In his eyes we are, and forever will be, invaluable. We no longer have to caricature, put others in their place, compete, or take sides in order to feel esteem for ourselves. In and through Jesus, we already are esteemed. What could be better than that?

LIVING OUTSIDE THE LINES

The secular response to the Christ story always goes like this: he was a great prophet, obviously a very interesting guy, had a lot to say along the lines of other great prophets, be they Elijah, Muhammad, Buddha, or Confucius. But actually Christ doesn't allow you that. He doesn't let you off that hook. . . . Either Christ was who He said He was—the Messiah—or a complete nutcase. I mean, we're talking nutcase on the level of Charles Manson. . . . I'm not joking here. The idea that the entire course of civilization for over half of the globe could have its fate changed and turned upside-down by a nutcase, for me, that's farfetched. . . . So I ask myself a question a lot of people have asked: Who is this man? And was He who He said He was, or was He just a religious nut? And there it is, and that's the question.

—BONO

As I said in the introduction, I wrote this book because I'm tired of taking sides. But sometimes taking sides is unavoidable.

When faced with Jesus' claim that he is "the way, and the truth, and the life," that no one comes to God the Father except through him,[1] we have to choose. Do we believe him—or not? Will we accept him—or not? Believing and receiving Jesus is what gives us the right to be part of God's family.[2] We are either part of his family or not part of his family.

In this sense, as far as Jesus is concerned, everyone will ultimately "take a side."

That's not to say that believers—those who have sided with Jesus—don't have doubts. Most of us do at one time or another. Several years into his career as a Presbyterian minister, Francis Schaeffer began to have *serious* doubts about his Christian faith. His doubts were triggered by a growing concern over how poorly the Christians he knew treated one another, especially in areas of disagreement. He witnessed a lot of negativity and faultfinding, as well as backbiting, gossip, manipulation, power plays, and underhandedness among his fellow ministers. He wrestled deeply with the question of how ministers could be so uncompromising about the Bible and its teachings about the grace, love, kindness, and forgiveness of God, yet be so harsh and ugly in their personal lives. It was out of this disillusionment that he one day confided in his wife, Edith,

> Edith, I feel really torn to pieces by the lack of reality, the lack of seeing the results the Bible talks about, which should be seen in the Lord's people. I'm not talking only about people I'm working with . . . but I'm not satisfied with myself. It seems that the only honest thing to do is to rethink, reexamine the whole matter of Christianity. Is it true? I need to go back to my agnosticism and start at the beginning.[3]

Schaeffer spent several months reading and rereading the Bible. He also immersed himself in philosophy as well as the writings of the various world religions. His goal was to put Christianity to the test and to see if it could withstand the scrutiny of comparison to every other plausible worldview. In the end, Schaeffer arrived back at the place where he had begun several years before, concluding that there is only one reason to be a Christian: not because it seems to make sense, or because it feels good, or because it is beautiful, but because it is true.[4]

Because it is true.

That's the conclusion I've come to as well.

Changed Minds and Changed Lives

I have to say that I'm in good company. The list of intellectual titans who are Christians is not a list of merely two or three. There are many throughout history who, having looked seriously and with an open mind into the claims of biblical Christianity, became Christians themselves. Jonathan Edwards, an early president of Princeton University and also a Christian minister and missionary, was identified by the *Encyclopedia Brittanica* as one of the brightest minds ever to set foot on American soil. Simon Greenleaf, chief founder of Harvard Law School and the author of the renowned legal work *A Treatise on the Law of Evidence*, set out to demonstrate that the resurrection of Jesus Christ was a made-up fairy tale, a hoax that could be believed only by ignorant, unenlightened fools—and concluded, as Schaeffer did, that there is only one reason to be a Christian: because it's true. Having arrived at this conclusion, Greenleaf, too, became a believer in Jesus. There are also committed believers within the ranks of the world's prominent scientists and philosophers, including Francis Collins, Galileo, Copernicus, and Pascal. Oxford historian C. S. Lewis, once an atheist who in his own words was "angry with God for not existing,"[5] became a Christian when his close friend J. R. R. Tolkien convinced him that the story of God's redemption of the world through Jesus is the Story behind every good story.

More recently, Jordan Monge, a lifelong atheist and political science major at Harvard, committed her life to Christ. From early childhood, Monge had gained a reputation for tearing down "poorly constructed arguments" that defended religion. Over time, however, thoughtful responses from Christian friends to her nonbelief pressed her to begin doubting her doubts. Increasingly, the way of Jesus began to become plausible to her. As she considered the cross of Jesus in particular, Christianity became not only plausible but also beautiful.[6] Other contemporary, bright, nonbelieving people who have become followers of Jesus include Kirsten Powers, a political news analyst who wrote about how she was converted from atheism to Christianity after discovering the overwhelming body of evidence for biblical truth,[7] and Malcolm Gladwell, journalist, author, speaker, and staff writer for the *New Yorker*.[8]

Other evidence for Christianity includes billions of lives over the centuries that have been changed. Liars becoming more honest; crooks returning what they have stolen; anxious and dying people finding peace; cowardly and fearful people finding courage; hurtful people asking forgiveness of those they have hurt; bodies wasting away as the souls who inhabit those bodies become more alive; businesspeople doing the less profitable thing because it is the right thing; aimless people finding meaning in their lives; spouses staying committed to each other through the hard and dry seasons; addicts becoming sober; adulterers becoming chaste; pregnant mothers continuing their pregnancies knowing that they are carrying a child with Down syndrome; rejected and unappreciated parents persisting in unconditional love toward their straying, entitled children; bereaved parents understanding that their greatest and most worthwhile task in life is to wrestle toward forgiving their beloved daughter's abductor and murderer . . . just as God, through Jesus, has forgiven them. These are only a few examples of how Jesus Christ changes people.

God's power—the same power that Christians believe spoke the galaxies into being, that parted the sea, that caused a blind man to see, that enabled a paralytic to get up and walk, and that raised Jesus from the dead—accounts for the billions of people who, having been brought into relationship with Jesus, have become better versions of themselves. "If anyone is in Christ, he is a new creation. The old has passed away; behold, the new has come."[9]

Perhaps you have been turned off of Christianity because of intellectual roadblocks. Perhaps, like Francis Schaeffer, your faith has taken a hit by the "lack of reality" that you perceive in the lives and behavior of Christians around you.

In the midst of your questions, doubts, and disappointments, are there any Christians in your life whose lives have shown you glimpses of something different, something more beautiful and lovely, even something admirable? Have you ever seen in Christians something that gave you pause about your doubts, that led you to consider that perhaps there is something to this Jesus character? Have you ever witnessed in Christians something that stirred a longing in you?

If so, could this be Jesus reaching out to you, inviting you to come live outside the lines with him?

If there are no such Christians in your life, and if there is no such longing, would you consider, as the Harvard student Jordan Monge did, investigating "the works of the masters" such as Augustine, Anselm, Aquinas, Descartes, Kant, Pascal, and Lewis? Better yet, would you consider reading through each of the four "Jesus biographies" in the Bible—the Gospels according to Matthew, Mark, Luke, and John—each written from the perspective of a first-century believer whose life had been made new by the life, death, burial, and resurrection of Jesus?[10]

> Are there any Christians in your life whose lives have shown you glimpses of something different, something more beautiful and lovely, even something admirable?

If you are not ready to open yourself to the possibility that Jesus is the truth, would you consider embarking on the journey that Simon Greenleaf once made? Would you accept the challenge, as he did, of attempting to prove that it is false?

Perhaps in your quest to prove Christianity to be false, you might discover, as Greenleaf and Schaeffer did, that there is only one reason to be a Christian: because it's true.

Or perhaps you won't.

Concluding Thoughts for Nonbelievers ... and Believers, Too

If you are a committed nonbeliever, there are two final thoughts I would like to share with you. First, congratulations! You have made it all the way through a book written by a Christian minister, a likely indication that you are a thoughtful, open-minded person willing to consider perspectives that are "outside the lines" of your own viewpoint. Thank you for being willing to consider ideas that matter deeply to me and also to others who, like me, believe that Jesus is the truth. If you are ever in Nashville on a Sunday, catch me after one of the services at Christ Presbyterian Church. I would love to hear your thoughts about what you have read in these pages.

Second, you may never believe the things that I and other Christians believe. If this proves to be the case, I understand. With all of the evidence that is there to support the truth claims of Christianity, we Christians must admit that our beliefs, though undergirded with evidence, are quite far-fetched to the human mind. After all, we believe that the hope of the universe rests on the shoulders of Jesus, a first-century Middle Eastern man who was conceived by a teenage virgin, born in an obscure town, and prone to hang out with people who were not religious and, for the most part, were unimpressive. He spent much of his adult life with no place to lay his head, and he died between two crooks on top of a trash heap. Admittedly, these details about Jesus' life don't exactly scream "the hope of the universe" or "Savior of the world." And yet, billions of people have believed it and surrendered their whole lives to its founder, leader, and king.

There are others, like Russian novelist Fyodor Dostoevsky, who came to believe that Christianity was not only the truth, but that it is also the most beautiful among all the alternatives: "This *Credo* is very simple, here it is: to believe that nothing is more beautiful, profound, sympathetic, reasonable, manly, and more perfect than Christ."[11]

But I digress.

To remain true to the purpose of this book, I will finish by stepping outside the lines a bit and share some advice with my fellow Christians. Interestingly, the advice comes from an essay called "Top 10 Tips for Christian Evangelism (From an Atheist)." The atheist writer's name is Daniel Fincke, and his advice is written especially for Christians. Whether you agree with every piece of his advice or not, I hope that you find it helpful. As for me, I find most of his advice to be, well . . . quite Christian.

1. **Be Like Jesus: Hang with the Sinners and Judge the Judgers.**
   The most admirable part of the story of Jesus, even to an atheist like me, . . . is the way that the Gospels portray him as a . . . preacher who focused his sermons against those who abused their wealth and religious power . . . while he spent his time hanging out with the outcasts loathed by his community.

2. **Form Genuine Relationships with People, Don't Treat Them as Projects.**
   Loving people should not be seen as a tool for getting access to someone so you can do your work fixing them.

Loving people means more than just saving them. If you're turning another person into a project, stop it. Treat them like your peer and not someone to be manipulated and shaped for their own good.

3. **Actions Speak Louder Than Words.**
People will figure out whether they like you, want to be close to you, or have anything to learn from you by how you behave, far more than by anything you say.

4. **When Talking about Religious and Philosophical Matters, Ask More Questions and Do Less Preaching.**
People just like to be heard and they like people who listen to them. And they will feel more trust *in* you the more that they open up *to* you. You have to overcome the temptation to make your attempts to persuade others all about how *you* feel and what you think. Your focus must be on what the person you're persuading feels and thinks.

5. **Don't Give Unsolicited Advice or Judgments. Support People and Wait for Them to Ask for Your Input If They Want It.**
Ask if they want your advice before giving it. . . . I think you have to trust that a morally perfect God can save people without you acting in exploitative and manipulative ways.

6. **Appreciate That Nominal Christians Are Christians Too.**
People are extremely complicated. If you are walking through the world categorizing everyone you meet into two categories—True Christians vs. The Unsaved—you are not only being shamefully judgmental, but you are risking alienating yourself from those you want to see saved.

7. **Don't Try to Force Others into Christian Participation.**
Don't be the Christian who tries . . . to turn your
entire common spaces—your workplace, your living
room, your school, your book club, your government,
etc.—into specifically Christian contexts. Don't try to
rope everyone into prayers or other acts of worship or
acknowledgment of Jesus. . . . Make it so all participation
in Christianity is *free and chosen* by *all* the participants.

8. **Understand Atheists and Embrace the Opportunity
Confrontational Atheists Afford You.**
Don't ignore our rational concerns, interests, and preoc-
cupations or you will be *wasting your time.* . . . When
you find one of us who is rather willing to have an argu-
ment with you, *be grateful we are interested in talking to
you about your faith.* Rejoice!

9. **Respect Other Religions Even As You Evangelize Their
Members**
Have confidence that if your faith is true and superior
that just comparing faiths in an in-depth way with
someone of a different faith will spark this realization,
without you having to present yourself as the enlightened one there to save others.[12]

And coming in at number ten:

10. **Love Your Enemies, Not Just Your Tribe.**[13]

ABOUT THE AUTHOR

SCOTT SAULS serves as senior pastor of Christ Presbyterian Church in Nashville, Tennessee. Previously, Scott was a lead and preaching pastor for Redeemer Presbyterian Church in New York City, where he served alongside Dr. Timothy Keller. Scott has also planted two churches—one in Kansas City, Kansas, and the other in St. Louis, Missouri. Scott is a frequent speaker at church conferences, leadership retreats, and to university students. Scott currently lives in Nashville with his wife, Patti, and his daughters, Abby and Ellie. Learn more about Scott on his blog at scottsauls.com or by following @scottsauls on Twitter.

NOTES

INTRODUCTION: JESUS OUTSIDE THE LINES

1. Tim Kreider, *We Learn Nothing: Essays and Cartoons* (New York: Simon & Schuster, 2012), 50–51.
2. See, for example, Timothy Keller's Facebook page, accessed October 10, 2014, https://www.facebook.com/TimKellerNYC/posts/747055218667700.
3. Matthew 5:43-48, NIV.
4. Romans 5:8, emphasis added.
5. See John 17.
6. See Galatians 3:28.
7. Matthew 7:24-27.
8. Chris Stedman, "Want to Talk to Non-Christians? Six Tips from an Atheist," Q Ideas, "Articles," accessed October 15, 2014, http://www.qideas.org /articles/want-to-talk-to-non-christians-six-tips-from-an-atheist/.
9. See Mark 10:17-27.
10. 1 Peter 3:15-16.
11. Shane Windmeyer, "Dan and Me: My Coming Out as a Friend of Dan Cathy and Chick-fil-A," *Huffington Post*, January 28, 2013, http://www.huffingtonpost.com/shane-l-windmeyer/dan-cathy-chick-fil-a _b_2564379.html.

CHAPTER 1: RED STATE OR BLUE STATE?

1. See Matthew 17:24-27.
2. See Romans 13:1-7; 1 Peter 2:17.
3. See Matthew 8:5-13.
4. Joshua 5:13-15.
5. See Matthew 10:3-4.
6. See Ephesians 2:14-16.

7. The entire account can be read in John 18:28-40.

8. John 18:37-38.

9. Ted Elliott, Terry Rossio, Joe Stillman, and Roger S. H. Schulman, *Shrek*, directed by Andrew Adamson and Vicky Jenson (Glendale, CA: DreamWorks Animation, 2001), Film.

10. Cathleen Falsani, "Marcus Mumford, Lead Singer of Mumford & Sons: 'I Wouldn't Call Myself a Christian,'" *Huffington Post*, April 3, 2013, http://www.huffingtonpost.com/2013/04/03/marcus-mumford-lead-singer -of-mumford--sons-i-wouldnt-call-myself-a-christian_n_3009777.html.

11. Matthew 5:18.

12. See Revelation 22:18-19; John 3:5.

13. See Matthew 5–7.

14. See Ephesians 2:11-22; Luke 4:18-21.

15. C. S. Lewis, *Mere Christianity*, revised and enlarged edition (New York: HarperOne, 2001), book 3, "Christian Behaviour," chapter 10, "Hope."

16. John 6:15.

17. Psalm 20:7; 146:3.

18. Acts 2:46-47.

19. Julian, *Letters* 22, trans. Wilmer C. Wright, Loeb Classical Library 157 (Cambridge, MA: Harvard University Press, 1923).

20. William Barclay, *The Letters to the Galatians and Ephesians*, 3rd ed. (Louisville, KY: Westminster John Knox Press, 2002), 203.

21. Matthew 6:33.

CHAPTER 2: FOR THE UNBORN OR FOR THE POOR?

1. Exodus 21:22 makes reference to a "woman with child" (KJV). The word "child" in the Hebrew (*yeled*) is the same Hebrew word that is used for a child outside the womb. In other words, the Scriptures do not distinguish between the personhood of a prenatal child and a postnatal child. In Psalm 139:13, the psalmist prays, "You knitted me together in my mother's womb." In Jeremiah 1:5, the Lord affirms to the prophet, "Before I formed you in the womb I knew you, and before you were born I consecrated you."

2. See, for example, Luke 4:16-21.

3. See Genesis 1:26-27.

4. Psalm 8:1, 3-5.

5. See Psalm 139:14.

6. See Romans 8:39.

7. See Jeremiah 29:11.

8. See John 3:16.

9. 1 John 3:19-21.

10. 2 Corinthians 4:6.

11. Matthew 5:43-47.

12. C. S. Lewis, *The Weight of Glory: And Other Addresses* (New York: HarperCollins, 2001), 45–46.

13. Isaiah 53:2-3.

14. Luke 18:16-17.

15. Gabe Lyons, "In Defense of Down Syndrome Children . . . Like My Son," *Huffington Post*, February 7, 2012, http://www.huffingtonpost.com /gabe-lyons/raising-children-with-down-syndrome_b_1260307.html, emphasis added.

16. 1 Corinthians 1:26-31.

17. See 2 Corinthians 8:9.

18. Luke 4:18-19.

19. Luke 4:21.

20. For an understanding of what I mean by "effective," you'll want to read *When Helping Hurts* by Steve Corbett and Brian Fikkert.

21. Deuteronomy 15:7-8, 11.

22. Acts 20:35.

23. John 3:16.

24. Joseph Hart, "Come Ye Sinners."

CHAPTER 3: PERSONAL FAITH OR INSTITUTIONAL CHURCH?

1. "A Faith Revolution Is Redefining 'Church,' According to New Study," Barna Group, October 10, 2005, https://www.barna.org/barna-update /5-barna-update/170-a-faith-revolution-is-redefining-qchurchq-according -to-new-study#.

2. See Acts 2:42-47.

3. Donald Miller, "I Don't Worship God by Singing. I Connect with Him Elsewhere," *Storyline* (blog), February 3, 2014, http://storylineblog .com/2014/02/03/i-dont-worship-god-by-singing-i-connect-with-him -elsewhere/.

4. Kelly Bean, *How to Be a Christian without Going to Church* (Ada, MI: Baker Books, 2014), 10, 36, 103, 112.

5. 1 Corinthians 10:31.

6. See 1 Corinthians 12:7; 1 John 3:1-2; John 10:16; 1 Timothy 3:1-13.

7. Hebrews 10:25.

8. Rick Warren, *The Purpose Driven Life: What on Earth Am I Here For?* expanded ed. (Grand Rapids, MI: Zondervan, 2012), 170–71.

9. "Anne Rice: 'Today I Quit Being a Christian,'" *Christianity Today*, "Gleanings," August 2, 2010, http://www.christianitytoday.com/gleanings/2010/august /anne-rice-today-i-quit-being-christian.html.

10. Justin McRoberts, "Open Letter to Anne Rice," accessed November 18, 2014, Justin McRoberts blog, http://justinmcroberts.com/blog/open-letter-to -anne-rice/.

11. See Revelation 21:1-3.

12. Romans 5:8, emphasis added.

13. D. A. Carson, *Love in Hard Places* (Wheaton, IL: Crossway, 2002), 61.

14. C. S. Lewis, *The Four Loves* (New York: Harcourt Books, 1991), 61–62.

15. See 1 Corinthians 12:21.

CHAPTER 4: MONEY GUILT OR MONEY GREED?

1. John 12:5, 7-8, NIV.
2. See, for example, Mark 10:25; Luke 12:15; 16:13; Matthew 6:19-20.
3. See Genesis 2:8-9; 13:2; Exodus 33:3; Joshua 1:7-8; 1 Kings 3:1-15; Job 1:1-8; Ecclesiastes 5:18-20; Psalm 144:12-14; Amos; Luke 4:16-19; 2 Corinthians 8:9; 1 Peter 1:4; John 14:2-3; Revelation 21.
4. See Numbers 18:20; Lamentations 3:24; Psalm 16:5; 2 Corinthians 12:7-10.
5. Philippians 4:11-13, emphasis added.
6. Sam Polk, "For the Love of Money," *New York Times*, January 18, 2014, http://www.nytimes.com/2014/01/19/opinion/sunday/for-the-love-of-money.html.
7. C. S. Lewis, *Mere Christianity*, revised and amplified edition (New York: HarperCollins, 2001), book 3, "Christian Behaviour," chapter 8, "The Great Sin."
8. See 1 Timothy 6:10; Matthew 7:5.
9. Juliet Schor, *The Overspent American* (New York: Harper Perennial, 1999), 17.
10. Madeline Levine, *The Price of Privilege* (New York: HarperCollins, 2006), 17.
11. Luke 12:15.
12. Luke 16:13.
13. 1 Timothy 6:8-10, emphasis added.
14. I am especially indebted to Dr. Anderson Spickard for these insights.
15. See Acts 20:35.
16. Luke 12:32-34 (see also verses 13-31).
17. In the Old Testament (see Malachi 3:6-12), God confronts the people of Israel for "robbing him" by withholding their tithes and offerings. The Hebrew word for *tithe* means "tenth," referring to the biblical pattern of returning the first 10 percent of one's income back to God (see Leviticus 27:32). In Old Testament times, the tithe was given in the form of regular contributions to the Temple treasury. The *offerings* were "above and beyond" contributions people made in addition to the tithe, and there were various kinds. In the New Testament, the principle of making regular contributions to the church is also encouraged (see 1 Corinthians 16:1-4). While Jesus affirms the tithe as a continuing principle (see Matthew 23:23; Luke 11:42), the New Testament appears to encourage an even more openhanded and generous way of life in response to the free and generous grace God has extended to us in the gospel. In the New Testament church, no one said that any of his belongings were his own (see Acts 4:32), Jesus praises a widow for her exemplary and over-the-top generosity (see Luke 21:1-4), and the wealthy are encouraged to be generous with their wealth and be content with basic needs being met—all because godliness with contentment is great gain, and the love of money is a root of all kinds of evil (see 1 Timothy 6:3-10).
18. Mike Holmes, "What Would Happen if the Church Tithed?" *Relevant*, July 10, 2013, http://www.relevantmagazine.com/god/church/what-would-happen-if-church-tithed.
19. Malachi 3:8-10, 12.

CHAPTER 5: AFFIRMATION OR CRITIQUE?
1. Both quotes from BrainyQuote.com, accessed October 25, 2014.
2. Philip Yancey, "Grace," Q&A on Philip Yancey's official website, 2009, accessed October 25, 2014, http://philipyancey.com/q-and-a-topics/grace.
3. Colossians 4:6.
4. See John 8:39-59; Matthew 23:1-36; Luke 15:1-2; Matthew 21:31.
5. Dan Allender, *How Children Raise Parents: The Art of Listening to Your Family* (Colorado Springs: WaterBrook Press, 2005), see especially chapter 1.
6. Donald Miller, *Searching for God Knows What* (Nashville: Thomas Nelson, 2004), 116.
7. See Luke 19:37-40; Isaiah 55:12.
8. Psalm 8:5-6.
9. See Isaiah 64:6.
10. See Matthew 16:13-19.
11. Mark 16:7, emphasis added.
12. John 4:9.
13. See John 8:1-11; Luke 7:36-50; Luke 10:25-37; 19:1-10.
14. Matthew 11:19.
15. American Chesterton Society, accessed October 29, 2014, http://www.chesterton.org/wrong-with-world/.
16. Proverbs 27:6; Psalm 141:5.
17. Galatians 6:1.
18. John 13:35, emphasis added.
19. Dietrich Bonhoeffer, *Life Together* (New York: HarperCollins, 1954), 30.
20. See 2 Corinthians 13:5; Luke 6:42.
21. 1 Corinthians 5:12-13.
22. James 3:9-10.

CHAPTER 6: ACCOUNTABILITY OR COMPASSION?
1. See Luke 9:51-56.
2. See Matthew 5:22.
3. See Ezekiel 2:1–3:3.
4. Jean-Paul Sartre, *Being and Nothingness* (New York: Open Road Media, 2012), e-book, part 3, chapter 1, "The Look."
5. Deborah Solomon, "The Good Daughter: Questions for Amy Tan," *New York Times*, August 8, 2008, http://www.nytimes.com/2008/08/10/magazine/10wwln-Q4-t.html.
6. Lynn Hirschberg, "The Misfit," *Vanity Fair*, April 1991.
7. Blaise Pascal, *Pensées*, number 398.
8. *Westminster Shorter Catechism*, Question 4.
9. See Genesis 1:26–3:24; Revelation 21:1-5.
10. See footnote on Psalm 8:5 (NIV) and also 1 John 3:2-3.
11. Revelation 22:14; see also Isaiah 9:7.
12. Revelation 22:15, 18-19.

13. *The Autobiography of Charles Darwin*, ed. Nora Barlow (New York: W. W. Norton, 1958), 87.

14. Miroslav Volf, *Exclusion and Embrace: A Theological Exploration of Identity, Otherness, and Reconciliation* (Nashville: Abingdon Press, 1996), Google e-book, chap. 7, "Violence and Peace."

15. Howard Thurman, as quoted in Timothy Keller, Redeemer Presbyterian Church, New York, *Timothy Keller Sermon Archive*, Logos Bible Software (2013).

16. Elie Wiesel, *Night* (New York: Hill and Wang, 2006), 68.

17. Rebecca Pippert, *Hope Has Its Reasons: The Search to Satisfy Our Deepest Longings*, rev. ed. (Downers Grove, IL: InterVarsity Press, 2001), 99–101.

18. See Ezekiel 18:23; Luke 9:51-55; 19:41-44; Matthew 9:36; Acts 9:1-19.

19. Romans 3:23.

20. See Isaiah 6:1-7.

21. Romans 8:1.

22. Matthew 3:7.

23. Larry Alex Taunton, "Listening to Young Atheists: Lessons for a Stronger Christianity," *Atlantic*, June 6, 2013, http://www.theatlantic.com/national /archive/2013/06/listening-to-young-atheists-lessons-for-a-stronger -christianity/276584/2/.

CHAPTER 7: HYPOCRITE OR WORK IN PROGRESS?

1. Homer Jack, ed., *The Gandhi Reader: A Sourcebook of His Life and Writings* (New York: Grove Press, 1994), 36.

2. Philip Yancey, *Soul Survivor* (New York: Random House LLC, 2002), Kindle edition.

3. Ibid.

4. Ibid.

5. Walker Percy, *The Second Coming* (New York: Macmillan, 1999), 188.

6. See Romans 3:23; 7:21-25; Isaiah 64:6.

7. See Galatians 5:22-23.

8. 1 Kings 15:11; 2 Kings 18:3.

9. Romans 7:8.

10. Quoted in Philip Yancey, "Message: A Sermon of Offense," *The Jesus I Never Knew* (Grand Rapids, MI: Zondervan, 2008), ePub format.

11. Nicholas Kristof, "Evangelicals without Blowhards," *New York Times*, July 30, 2011, http://www.nytimes.com/2011/07/31/opinion/sunday/kristof -evangelicals-without-blowhards.html?_r=0 nytimes.com, emphasis added.

12. Jesse Carey, "6 Unexpected Faith Conversations from Pop Culture," *Relevant*, "Culture," May 6, 2014, http://www.relevantmagazine.com/culture/6 -unexpected-faith-conversations-pop-culture.

13. 1 Corinthians 10:13-14, 31; 11:1.

14. Anne Lamott, "On Meaning, Hope, and Repair" (lecture presented at the Festival of Faith and Writing, Grand Rapids, MI, April 11, 2014).

15. Galatians 5:22-24.

16. 1 Corinthians 6:9-11.
17. Acts 4:13.
18. See 1 Corinthians 11:1.

CHAPTER 8: CHASTITY OR SEXUAL FREEDOM?
1. Randall Patterson, "Students of Virginity," *New York Times*, March 30, 2008, http://www.nytimes.com/2008/03/30/magazine/30Chastity-t.html.
2. Mark Oppenheimer, "Married, With Infidelities," *New York Times*, June 30, 2011, http://www.nytimes.com/2011/07/03/magazine/infidelity-will-keep-us -together.html.
3. See Matthew 19:4-5 quoting Genesis 1:27 and 2:24; Exodus 20:14; Proverbs 5:15-20; 7:16-23; 1 Corinthians 6:16; Hebrews 13:4.
4. http://www.familysafemedia.com/pornography_statistics.html; http://www.cnbc.com/id/45989346.
5. Frank Rich, "Naked Capitalists," *New York Times*, May 20, 2001, http://www.nytimes.com/2001/05/20/magazine/naked-capitalists.html.
6. Naomi Wolf, "The Porn Myth," *New York Magazine*, October 29, 2003, http://nymag.com/nymetro/news/trends/n_9437/.
7. Gary Brooks, quoted in Pamela Paul, *Pornified* (New York: Times Books, 2005), 80.
8. Jan Hoffman, "Bingeing on Celebrity Weight Battles," *New York Times*, May 29, 2009, http://www.nytimes.com/2009/05/31/fashion/31fat.html.
9. Genesis 2:24-25.
10. Proverbs 5:15, 18-19.
11. See 1 Corinthians 7:1-5.
12. Hosea 2:19.
13. Isaiah 62:5.
14. See Revelation 19:9; 21:1-5.
15. Dietrich Bonhoeffer, *The Cost of Discipleship* (New York: Touchstone, 1995), 89.
16. Luke 14:33.
17. See Genesis 1:27; 5:2; Matthew 19:4-5.
18. Proverbs 16:25.
19. See Leviticus 18:22; Romans 1:26-27; 1 Corinthians 6:9-10; 1 Timothy 1:8-11.
20. See Philemon 1:15-17, NIV.
21. F. F. Bruce, *Paul: Apostle of the Heart Set Free* (Grand Rapids, MI: Eerdmans, 1977), 400–401.
22. See Matthew 16:24; Luke 9:23.
23. Matthew 23:2-4.
24. 2 Samuel 1:26.
25. See 1 Samuel 18:1.
26. Here I am indebted to C. S. Lewis's idea of "naked personalities" in *The Four Loves*.
27. Wesley Hill, *Washed and Waiting: Reflections on Christian Faithfulness and Homosexuality* (Grand Rapids, MI: Zondervan, 2010), 95.
28. See Psalm 68:6; Mark 10:29-30; Genesis 2:18.

29. Ephesians 5:32.
30. See Ephesians 5:21-33.
31. See Matthew 22:30; Revelation 19:6-8.
32. Paige Benton, "Singled Out by God for Good," *PCPC Witness*, February 1998, http://static.pcpc.org/articles/singles/singledout.pdf.

CHAPTER 9: HOPE OR REALISM?
1. Psalm 13:1.
2. Psalm 22:1.
3. See Romans 5:4.
4. See Job 1:1-20.
5. Job 1:21.
6. Job 2:9.
7. Job 9:21-23.
8. See Revelation 21:1-5.
9. C. S. Lewis, *A Grief Observed* (New York: HarperOne, 2009), 17–18.
10. Psalm 22:1-2.
11. Psalm 13:1-2.
12. John 11:21.
13. John 11:32.
14. Deuteronomy 29:29.
15. 1 Corinthians 13:12.
16. John 11:37.
17. John 11:25-26.
18. See John 11:35.
19. Isaiah 53:3-5, 9-12.
20. John 11:33, 38.
21. Nicholas Wolterstorff, *Lament for a Son* (Grand Rapids, MI: Eerdmans, 1987), 80–81.
22. See John 11:25.
23. Flannery O'Connor, *The Habit of Being: Letters of Flannery O'Connor*, ed. Sally Fitzgerald (New York: Farrar, Straus and Giroux, 1988), 100.
24. See Romans 6:23; Genesis 2:17.
25. John 11:23, 25-26.
26. Revelation 21:1-5.
27. C. S. Lewis, *The Great Divorce* (New York: HarperCollins, 2001), 69.
28. See 1 Corinthians 13:12.
29. See John 11:41-44.
30. C. S. Lewis, *Mere Christianity* (New York: HarperOne, 2001), 37–38.
31. Exodus 3:14.

CHAPTER 10: SELF-ESTEEM OR GOD-ESTEEM?
1. C. S. Lewis, *Mere Christianity* (New York: Touchstone, 1996), 109–12.
2. Luke 18:11-12.

3. Miroslav Volf, *Exclusion and Embrace* (Nashville, TN: Abingdon Press, 1996), 124.
4. Patty Lee, "Kelly Osbourne: 'I Took More Hell for Being Fat' Than for Being a Drug Addict," *New York Daily News*, February 24, 2010, http://www.nydailynews.com/entertainment/gossip/kelly-osbourne-hell-fat-drug-addict-article-1.172358.
5. Philippians 2:3, NIV.
6. Chris Evert, as quoted in Timothy Keller, *Counterfeit Gods* (New York: Penguin, 2009), 77.
7. Heidi Grant Halvorson, "To Succeed, Forget Self-Esteem," *Harvard Business Review*, September 20, 2012, https://hbr.org/2012/09/to-succeed-forget-self-esteem/.
8. See Psalm 17:8; 139:14; Zephaniah 3:17; John 10:28-29; Romans 3:23; 5:8; 8:1-2, 14-15, 38-39.
9. See Philippians 2:3.
10. See Romans 8:1, 38-39.
11. See Matthew 1:1-16; Luke 3:23-38.
12. Job 19:25-26.

EPILOGUE: LIVING OUTSIDE THE LINES

1. John 14:6.
2. See John 1:12.
3. Jerram Barrs, "Francis Schaeffer: The Man and His Message," *Thistle*, Covenant Seminary, October 24, 2012, www.covenantseminary.edu/the-thistle/francis-schaeffer-the-man-and-his-message/.
4. Michael Maudlin, "Midwives of Francis Schaeffer" *Christianity Today*, March 3, 1997, http://www.christianitytoday.com/ct/1997/march3/7t3006.html.
5. C. S. Lewis, "Light and Shade," chap. 7 in *Surprised by Joy*.
6. You can read Jordan Monge's story in her article "The Atheist's Dilemma," *Christianity Today*, April 4, 2013, http://www.christianitytoday.com/ct/2013/march/atheists-dilemma.html.
7. See Kirsten Powers, "Fox News' Highly Reluctant Jesus Follower," *Christianity Today*, October 22, 2013, http://www.christianitytoday.com/ct/2013/november/fox-news-highly-reluctant-jesus-follower-kirsten-powers.html.
8. See Malcolm Gladwell, "How I Rediscovered Faith," *Relevant*, January/February, 2014, www.relevantmagazine.com/culture/books/how-i-rediscovered-faith.
9. 2 Corinthians 5:17.
10. If you're interested in learning more about the evidence in support of the Christian faith, try one of these books: *Who Moved the Stone?* by Frank Morison, *The Case for Christ* and *The Case for Faith* by Lee Strobel, *More Than a Carpenter* and *Evidence That Demands a Verdict* by Josh McDowell, and *The Reason for God* by Timothy Keller.
11. Joseph Frank, *Dostoevsky: A Writer in His Time* (Princeton, NJ: Princeton Press, 2009), 220.

12. Daniel Fincke, "Top 10 Tips for Christian Evangelism (From an Atheist)," *Camels with Hammers* (blog), April 10, 2014, www.patheos.com/blogs/camelswithhammers/2014/04/top-10-tips-for-christian-evangelizing-from-an-atheist/.

13. Fincke, "Top 10 Tips."